THE
DARK SIDE
OF THE
MARKETPLACE

The Plight of the American Consumer

Senator Warren G. Magnuson
and Jean Carper

Prentice-Hall, Inc.
Englewood Cliffs, New Jersey

The Dark Side of the Marketplace:
The Plight of the American Consumer
by Senator Warren G. Magnuson and Jean Carper
© 1968 by Warren G. Magnuson and Jean Carper

First PRISM PAPERBACK edition, 1972

ISBN: 0-13-197186-7
Library of Congress Catalog Card Number: 68-20369

Printed in the United States of America
10   9   8   7   6   5   4   3   2   1

Prentice-Hall International, Inc., London
Prentice-Hall of Australia, Pty. Ltd., Sydney
Prentice-Hall of Canada, Ltd., Toronto
Prentice-Hall of India Private Ltd., New Delhi
Prentice-Hall of Japan, Inc., Tokyo

*This book is
dedicated to the
American consumer and to
the millions of ethical
and responsible
American businessmen.*

Contents

v

Introduction

When this book was first written—in 1967—the modern consumer revolt had barely begun to erupt. A handful of pioneers had warned of the snares and inequities in the marketplace: Senator Philip Hart, through the Antitrust Subcommittee, had exposed deceptive supermarket packaging and labeling and auto insurance abuses; Senator Paul Douglas for years had hammered away at credit abuses; Senator Maurine Neuberger had attacked cigarette advertising; and Ralph Nader, a fierce new citizen-voice, had forced an indifferent public to face the immorality of hazardous automobile design, giving thrust to passage of the Auto Safety Act of 1966. Of course, there had been consumer protection laws through the years, such as those governing hazardous substances and flammable fabrics, which we had developed in the Senate Commerce Committee.

But "consumerism" was yet to take root as a popular concept; its future was uncertain, although many of us were convinced its growth was inevitable. All of that has radically changed. Today the consumer movement is regarded as one of the most significant of the century. Hardly anyone is unaware of it. Consumer advocates, once considered "untouchables" by the media, now appear on the covers of national magazines. Businessmen, some of whom at first

1

derided the consumer movement, now take it seriously and often exploit it in their advertising. Most importantly, the consumer's consciousness has been raised, creating a new intolerance for shoddy, deceptive, or irresponsible practices by business. We no longer accept our status as the passive objects of confused pricing and misleading advertising which hamper our ability to make sound choices. The consumer asks: Why shouldn't I know how fresh a carton of milk or eggs is? Why shouldn't I be able to compare the cost of pounds and ounces of various products? Why shouldn't advertisements give me more than catch jingles and unsubstantiated claims so I can judge the best value, best suited to my purposes?

Moreover, the consumer movement has vastly expanded its scope, from sales deceptions and safety standards to concern over the environment—air and water pollution—and the ominous trend toward economic concentration which threatens consumers' welfare.

And it has become much better organized, its concern institutionalized, as not only individuals but groups—both new and old—take up the banner of the consumer with vigor. Newly formed public-interest law firms are advocating consumer reforms as vigorously as their counterparts in industry oppose them. Citizen-supported groups, such as John Gardner's Common Cause have sprung up. Even traditional consumer champions, such as the cooperative league and progressive unions have become noticeably more aggressive and have banded together through the broad-based Consumer Federation of America to keep up with the energy of the new consumer advocacy.

Congress—with members now more sensitive to the needs of consumers—has responded by intensifying legislative activities on behalf of consumers. Since I first came to Congress in 1936, I have seen the national concern over consumer protection greatly accelerate. In 1938, we extended the jurisdiction of the Federal Trade Commission to empower it specifically to prevent consumer deception. That same year we passed the Food, Drug and Cosmetic Act. After a period of dormancy during World War II, consumer protection efforts were renewed. In 1953, we passed the Flammable Fabrics Act, outlawing explosively flammable fabrics used in wearing apparel. Soon afterward came legislation requiring that refrigerator doors be designed to be opened from the inside, preventing children's entrapment. With the Kefauver-Harris Drug Amendments, we had in 1962 significant reforms in the labeling of prescription drugs and the testing of new drugs. About that same time Senator Paul Douglas introduced the first consumer credit reform law, calling for "truth in lending," a disclosure of finance rates in percentages. This bill did not pass until 1967.

Then there were the landmark laws setting minimum safety standards for tires and automobiles which we passed in 1966. Later the Fair Packaging and Labeling Act, the Child Protection Act, the Gas Pipeline Safety Act, the Toy Safety Act, and the unprecedented ban on broadcast cigarette advertising, all of which bear the imprint of our Committee.

As this is written, we are approaching the legislative moment of truth on new major consumer and environmental reforms: national no-fault insurance legislation, sweeping federal product safety regulation to replace the patchwork quality of feeble state and federal legislation, warranty reforms, and our effort to give meaningful new enforcement tools to the Federal Trade Commission.

Increasingly concerned about the impact of new chemicals and other products on consumers of future generations, we have been developing toxic chemicals legislation. We are also seeking new modes of consumer self-help: consumer and environmental class action bills to enable the individual citizen to free himself of dependence upon weak or overburdened bureaucracies by seeking recourse in the courts. We are on the threshold of passing legislation to establish an independent consumer agency—a strong consumer lobby with the resources and authority to battle the corporate giants in the arena of government regulation, an arena in which the consumer has thus far been defenseless.

And yet, there is still bitter truth in the French adage "the more things change, the more they remain the same." In rereading this book for revision, from the vantage point of 1971, it was striking to me to see that the basic problems discussed herein still exist. Our new laws, reach only a fraction of the evils and too many good laws are yet to be effectively enforced.

The same frauds, as outlined in chapter 1, are still being per-
petrated on people nationwide. Many states still lack stringent
laws and enforcement. Garnishment of wages, though reformed
through truth-in-lending legislation, still entraps buyers. Quack
devices are still being sold, and the legislation called for in the
book has not been passed to prevent their getting on the market.
Legitimate medical devices, used primarily by surgeons, have become
an even bigger problem, but are still uncontrolled as to quality or
safety.

Unsafe products still flood the market, as recently documented
by the National Commission on Product Safety, and particularly,
flammable children's clothing is still the threat it was. Perhaps nowhere has the situation been less alleviated than with the poor
who are still oppressed by outmoded credit laws against which they
have little defense.

The names, dates, and certain facts may have changed. But, un-
happily, the story is the same.

The first edition of this book was introduced with these words:
"When this book was begun, I had some realization of how poorly
the American consumer is protected and how he is exploited by
the unscrupulous and irresponsible few of the business community.
But I, probably like most, had not fully felt the depth of the problem: its serious social consequences, its detrimental effect on ethical
business, its viciousness among the poor, its threat to human life:
in short, its true cancerous qualities in the fiber of American life.

"It is my firm conviction that the consumer, too, would be
shocked and surprised if he knew how inadequately protected he
is, how lax we have been in guaranteeing fair play and justice between buyer and seller."

Despite our progress, the situation, I believe, is still shocking,
perhaps even more so, for our expectations today are higher.

The reader will not find in this book a comprehensive discussion
of everything that has happened in the consumer movement since
the first writing in 1967; that obviously would require a separate
book, and several have been written in specialized areas; air and
water pollution, food adulteration, corporate responsibility. These
subject outgrowths of the original consumer movement are not

touched upon in this book. What the reader will find is a thoroughly updated version of the subject matter of the original manuscript, a chronicle of deceptions and hazards in that "dark side of the marketplace." I like to think the material is, as New York magazine called it, "the classic exposé of consumer frauds and hazards," and that it provides a foundation for understanding the deception and irresponsibility in the marketplace which have given rise to a consumer revolution.

There are many people who contributed substantially to the making of this book with their ideas, information, critical reading of the manuscript and suggestions for revisions. I would like to acknowledge and thank the following: former commissioners Mary Gardiner Jones and Philip Elman of the Federal Trade Commission; Gale P. Gotschall, assistant general counsel of the FTC; Esther Peterson and Betty Furness, both former special assistants to the president for consumer affairs; Barnett Levy, director of the New York Bureau of Consumer Frauds and Protection; the staffs of the consumer protection bureaus of the attorneys general in Illinois, Washington and Ohio; the Neighborhood Legal Services lawyers throughout the country; the Consumers' Education and Protective Association of Philadelphia; Dr. David Caplovitz, associate professor of sociology at Columbia University; Congresswoman Leonor Sullivan; Thomas C. Roberts, Council of Better Business Bureaus; William V. White, director of the Division of Product Safety, Food and Drug Administration; Dr. Joseph Davis, director of medical devices of the FDA's Bureau of Drugs; Irene Bartlett, American Cancer Society, Jerry Walsh, Arthritis Foundation; Henry B. Montague, chief postal inspector, Post Office Department; Charles Miller, director of Fraud and Mailability Division, Post Office Department; David Swankin, director of the Washington office of Consumers Union; Morris Kaplan, technical director, Consumers Union; the staff of the Senate Commerce Committee; my co-author, Joan Carper; and my wife, Jermaine, one of the best informed and most outspoken consumer advocates I know.

Senator Warren G. Magnuson
November 1971

PART ONE

Chapter 1

Caveat Emptor

One evening two men in a Cadillac paid a call on an elderly couple in a small town in Arkansas. One of the men, a Mr. G., president of the Superior Improvement Company in Little Rock, presented himself to the couple as an important executive affiliated with Alcoa Aluminum Company. He told the couple that after a careful examination of their house he had chosen it to be a model home as part of a new advertising campaign to sell aluminum siding. Photographs, he said, would be taken of the house "before" and "after" the siding was applied and would be featured in beautiful brochures. Salesmen would bring prospective customers to view the house, and for every sale made as a result, Mr. G. promised to give the couple a commission of $100. When urged to sign an agreement, the couple protested that their house was old and they were thinking of using their savings to rebuild. But the promises of Mr. G. were irresistible. He asserted he was giving them the siding at $1,000 below cost, cheaper than they could get it anywhere, and that with the commissions their house would be transformed into a showplace of beauty for virtually nothing. "Well, then, he said one thing that kind of struck me," the homeowner later recalled. "He said to say a little prayer and pray to the Lord and let Him guide us as to whether to sign the contract." Touched by this display of humility, the man and woman signed a contract for $1,480 and gave Mr. G. a down-payment check for $200.

By the next morning, the couple was no longer so spellbound by Mr. G's promises. Skeptical, they checked around and discovered they could buy aluminum siding for much less than Mr. G.'s "bargain factory prices." The homeowner, realizing he had been fleeced, tried to stop payment on the check, but was told that one of Mr. G.'s representatives had been there that morning as the bank opened and cashed the check. Repeated attempts to reach Mr. G. by phone at his Little Rock office were futile. He was always "out," and, said the homeowner, "his secretary kind of laughed like it was a big joke." Finally, in desperation and worry over his wife's ill health, which had been aggravated by the transaction, the man borrowed money from a bank and paid off the bill in full. He was informed by a lawyer that if he refused to make payments, the finance company Mr. G. had sold the contract to could sue him—and collect. The workmen had already tacked up the siding, such as it was. And the contract he had signed was legally binding, regardless of the verbal misrepresentations.

Hundreds of persons in rural Arkansas, Tennessee, and Kentucky, since 1960, have been seduced by Mr. G.'s prayers and phony promises into paying exorbitant prices for shoddy workmanship and poor quality materials. Mr. G. claimed his aluminum was manufactured by Alcoa, Kaiser, or Reynolds Aluminum Company; it was in truth an off-brand, most of it shipped from Illinois. He told customers that it would "never chip, crack, fade, or soak up water, would never need paint, and had a lifetime guarantee." To many a homeowner's dismay, the siding was not applied by "factory-trained personnel" as promised, but sometimes by local teenagers. It fell off; the caulking was not done properly; the upper layer of finish could be rubbed off with the sweep of a hand. Some homes were left unfinished, aluminum and trash piled high in the yard. One man's house was such a shambles within a year, pockmarked by the fallen siding, that he needed a completely new siding job. The only thing he had bought from Mr. G. was a $2,400 debt.

Mr. G. and his salesmen preyed shamelessly on the illiterate, the poor, the old, and the guileless. One man said Mr. G.'s salesmen kept him up most of the night begging him to sign a note; weary and fatigued, he finally did. An elderly Negro was coerced into putting his X mark on a contract. Many were induced to part with their pensions and social security checks. Others said they were tricked into signing mortgages on their homes, and one couple swore their names were forged to a promissory note. In this brutal marketplace, there was no compunction about tacking aluminum siding on a shack in the fork of a dust-covered road and proclaiming it a "showplace."

Many people understood that because of the $100 bonus, they would have to pay little or nothing for the siding. Instead, once their names were on the contract, few homeowners ever saw Mr. G. or any of his salesmen again. No one brought prospective customers to view the renovated house as the salesmen had promised. Some people waited and waited, actually stayed home for days on end, fearing to leave the house, waiting for the customers that never came, until their hope turned to anguish.

Many were left with disastrous debts. A young schoolteacher signed a contract with a total price of $3,650. By the time monthly payments were figured out—eighty-four of them at $73.45 each—he discovered he had agreed to pay $6,132 over a period of seven years. Horrified, he borrowed money from his credit union and managed to persuade the finance company to let him pay off the debt; the company insisted, however, that he pay them more than $1,000 interest for use of the money for "less than a month."

Another couple signed a contract with Mr. G. for what they thought was about $2,000 and a mortgage on their house. Said a government lawyer: "When they sat down that night and in their sober judgment figured out what that was going to cost them over a period of eighty-four months—eighty-four payments—they were not going to pay $2,000; it would be some $4,000 to $4,400. That fellow attempted to commit suicide." Another pensioned purchaser came home and found his elderly wife unconscious on the bed. She recovered but confessed she had been so worried over the transaction with Mr. G. and the prospect of losing their home that she drank Lysol.

Early in 1964, the Federal Trade Commission issued a complaint against Mr. G. and his company, charging him with a dozen "unfair and deceptive practices." After hearings, he was ordered by the FTC to stop using such sales practices in interstate commerce. Mr. G. chose to take his case through the courts, and finally in early 1967, when the Supreme Court refused to hear his case, he was forced to comply with the FTC ruling. (It is interesting to note that the primary basis for Mr. G.'s defense was not innocence of deceptive selling, for he admitted that he had promised bonuses to prospective buyers. His main contention was that he was not engaging in interstate commerce and that, therefore, the FTC had no jurisdiction over his actions. The FTC can intervene only when it can be proved that a misdoer is operating across state lines.)

It might appear that such a ruling forced Mr. G. to stop using his lucrative, deceptive sales pitches (his annual volume of business was estimated at $400,000). On the contrary, he mapped out for the FTC his blueprint for future business: he would not advertise in interstate newspapers or other media, would not use the mails to send out brochures, and would not make sales to residents in other states. In other words, he pledged not to work his deceptive arts on anyone, except, of course, the unlucky prospects he might find within the borders of Arkansas.

According to complaints received by the Better Business Bureau in Little Rock, his salesmen remained active in Arkansas, using misrepresentations and "questionable advertising selling practices" to unload shoddy jobs and merchandise at unconscionable prices. Who was to stop him?

Although the Federal Trade Commission was reluctant to admit it, for fear of seeming to condone deceptive practices, the sorry truth in the matter was that as long as Mr. G.'s corporation scrupulously avoided interstate commerce, it could operate with impunity, free from FTC jurisdiction or intervention, no matter how blatantly dishonest the sales practices or how appalling to human sensibilities the amount of human misery left in their wake.

What about authorities in Arkansas? They, when alerted to this company's intention to hide behind state lines out of the reach of the FTC, wanted to take measures to protect the residents of Arkansas. But they did not have the necessary legislation. At that time they had no comprehensive law covering deceptive selling. They had only a variety of laws forbidding the use of deceptive practices to sell specific products, but aluminum siding was not among them.

It is true that Arkansas, like other states, had criminal fraud and false pretenses statutes, resulting in fines or imprisonment for those adjudged guilty. But these statutes are often a poor vehicle for preventing deceptive selling. Indictments under the statutes are exceedingly rare and convictions even rarer. It was not until July 1971, that Arkansas had on the books a comprehensive law, enabling their enforcement authorities to stop a variety of deceptive practices of the kind used by Mr. G.

Although this case is one of the most dramatic on record of how deceptive sellers can operate, it is hardly unique. Consumer deception flourishes nearly everywhere in the country, quite often unimpeded—and sometimes even abetted—by the law. As Helen Nelson, former consumer counsel for the governor of California, has said: "More money is being taken from Americans at penpoint than at gunpoint and the pen often makes it legal."

Deceptive selling by the unscrupulous few in the business underworld is, in fact, our most serious form of theft. It cheats Americans of several billion dollars yearly, more than is lost through robbery, burglary, larceny, auto theft, embezzlement, and forgery combined. Unlike the con men of yesterday who were often so heavy-handed that they offended the law, today's modern bandits of the marketplace are the masters of the light touch. With their insidious misrepresentations, silver-tongued lies, half-truths, and exaggerated promises, these men can reach even deeper into our pockets without producing a rustle to disturb the law, or often the victim himself. From coast to coast we are exposed to their Pandora's box of selling tricks—some old, but handily adapted to modern circumstances, and some new, carefully devised to outwit the law.

Although these schemes are staggering in scope and diverse in their nature (the Better Business Bureau has identified 800 different varieties), they invariably have several things in common: they are lucrative, they are subtle, and their purveyors rarely come in conflict with the law. According to a nationwide survey for the President's Commission on Law Enforcement and Administration of Justice in 1966, nine out of every ten victims of consumer fraud do not even bother to report it to the police. Fifty percent of the victimized felt they had no right or duty to complain; 40 percent believed the authorities could not be effective or would not want to be bothered; 10 percent were confused about where to report.

It is startling to consider that the vast majority of Americans victimized by consumer fraud feel that the law can or will do nothing to help them; but it is even more startling to realize that in many instances those victims are absolutely correct. Our legal remedies against consumer deception and fraud, some of which were adequate fifty, even twenty, years ago, are now so outdated as to leave the consumer nearly helpless. Under our present laws, with rare exceptions, we neither give relief to the victimized consumer nor effectively halt the swindlers.

The scheme so successfully used by Mr. G. is but one of five major schemes on which today's pyramid of deceptive selling rests. Although Mr. G. combined several techniques, his primary deception consisted of convincing homeowners that by making their home a "model," he was giving them "a special low price." (The phony "special price" is also used to sell a variety of items, including encyclopedias, automobiles, carpeting, roofing, and jewelry.) According to the Federal Trade Commission, the four other schemes that are currently most responsible for fleecing American consumers are *bait and switch advertising,* including "lo-balling," *chain-referral selling,* the *free gimmick,* and the *fear-sell.*

Of these, the most troublesome to detect and curtail is bait and switch advertising, in which the merchant advertises goods *which he has no intention of selling* in order to switch the prospective buyer to another item, invariably higher priced and with a greater margin of profit. Not only is bait advertising perfectly legal in many states, but it is so subtle that most victims are never aware that they have been deceived. We all see bait advertising continually, but probably few of us are aware of its insidious calculated nature.

Typically, this is the way the scheme works. A housewife in Alexandria, Virginia, noticed this advertisement in the classified section of a newspaper:

> SEW MACH.—1965 Singer
> Touch and Sew ***
> Reposs. Balance. $86.40
> New Mach. Guar. Dealer,
> Credit Dept. ***

When the salesman arrived at her home, following her telephone call to the company, she was appalled by the machine he carried. He set it down on the table and said: "Well, this is the machine." It was not the new one described in the ad. Rather, as the woman put it, it was "an old beaten-up Singer about twenty-five or thirty years old. . . . I'd seen machines in better shape at rummage sales." It was battered, scratched, and was a straight-stitch machine with no attachments. "I wouldn't have given more than $5 or $6 for it," she said. Noting her disappointment and admitting his "mistake," the salesman saved the day. He rushed to his car and brought in two sparkling, new, off-brand sewing machines priced at $289 and $365. The housewife chose the one for $289 and was given a discount because it was the "salesman's first day."

There were several glaring misrepresentations, designed to lure prospective customers, in this advertisement. The words "Reposs." (ostensibly standing for repossession) and "Balance" led the readers to believe the machines had been partially paid for by a previous purchaser and thus were being offered for a song. The signature "Credit Dept." created the same impression. In truth, the use of the Singer name was only a lure to support a full-time business of selling off-brand machines. This was proved by the fact that the dealer sold only two or three Singers a month, but spent $400 per month advertising them. Almost the total volume of his business was in the less well-known brand, the more expensive model to which customers were "switched."

Sometimes the salesman actually produced the advertised recent-model Singer, but then actively disparaged the "bait" by finding fault with it: "This machine is delicate and not functioning as it should." "We get a lot of complaints on these Singers." In most other instances, as in the case of the Alexandria housewife, the bait was so offensive that it had "built-in dissuaders," and prospects rejected it on sight. The way was then cleared for the salesman's pitch on the more profitable merchandise. In describing the subtlety of the approach, an FTC lawyer noted: "The prospective purchaser is led on without suspecting the insincerity of the salesman's presentation, and the switch is made to the higher-priced machine of a different make as though the transition were the suggestion of the prospect and not the salesman."

This unfair and deceptive advertising of a product without intent to sell goes on incessantly, with all kinds of merchandise: vacuum cleaners, television sets, carpeting, automobiles, radios, washing machines, furniture. Nor is it confined to door-to-door selling. For some stores, "bait and switch" advertising is the mainstay of their business. An appliance store advertises, for example, a 17-inch-screen TV for $99, but woe to the salesman who actually sells it. Said one store manager, referring to an advertised GE portable, "Any guy who lets that set go out the door goes with it." This merchandise is, in sales lingo, "nailed to the floor," and it is the salesman's job to knock it, to disparage it in any way, and to switch the customer to a more expensive model.

In an exclusive series of articles for *Home Furnishings Daily,* an anonymous salesman confessed that his store in New York City periodically featured phony special items in the newspaper, "to pull the shoppers in." He described the sale items: "First special in the ad is a 21-inch console television for $66. This always is a floor sample of ancient vintage and requires an aerial antenna of greater power than we have in the store to bring in a picture. Second special in the ad is a 10-cubic-foot refrigerator for $199. It is a make produced by a manufacturer swallowed up several mergers back. The color of the box might be described as an off-white with a slight tendency toward yellow. The guarantee on the unit is for six months.

Third bargain special is a famous-make 9-pound washer for $99. We have a beautiful wringer-type washer to show those attracted by this item, but strangely enough most of those attracted somehow assumed we were referring to a fully automatic washer in the ad. Completing our quartet is a 36-inch range for $65. There is really nothing striking about this stove unless it be the fact that it is two-tone in color with the sides being black. It has no oven heat control and a speck of rust has begun to appear in the chips in the enamel on top. After a customer has viewed any of the above mentioned specials, it is quite natural that he will ask to see something a bit better. With the step-up, comes my chance to make a sale at a good price."

A variation of bait advertising is lo-balling, a term that apparently originated several years ago and is used widely by auto mechanics. In lo-balling, the company advertises or promises a service at an outrageously low price and actually performs the work at the advertised price, but only as an enticement to get possession of the automobile (lo-balling to date has been almost exclusively associated with automobiles) so the company can gouge the owner for additional unneeded repairs.

The lucrative routine goes this way, as illustrated by the experience of a man in Washington, D.C. He responded to an advertisement promising to reseal his car's transmission for labor charges of $22 plus an extra charge for needed parts. He was promised one-day service. When he left the car, it was functioning properly except for an oil leakage, which was to be corrected by resealing the transmission.

"About 4:15 the same day, I went back and they had a transmission lying on a work bench, and they said: 'This is your transmission and here are some parts of metal that were found in it and the pump is completely shot and needs replacing.' So I talked to the manager and said, 'What will that cost?' He said, 'Well, it would cost about another $42,' which raised the cost of the job to about $76.

"So I told him to go ahead with it, take the things that were torn down if they needed a new pump, to put it in. He said it would be ready the next afternoon.

"Well, I called the next morning to find out if the car would be ready and he examined it further and said: 'All the bushings are shot and need replacing.' I said, 'What is that going to cost?' He said, 'Well, the total job is now $107.' "

Through this technique, lo-ballers have been known to run the price on transmission repairs up to $400 and $500.

The franchises of the Aamco Transmission Company, which used to sponsor television commercials starring actress Zsa Zsa Gabor, are accused of building their multimillion dollar business on lo-balling.

In Columbia, South Carolina, for example, three officers and employees of the local Aamco franchise were charged with conspiring to obtain money under false pretenses after a carefully marked 1959 automobile was left with them by state investigators for repairs. The transmission had previously been rebuilt, the parts marked by a competent mechanic, and was in good working order. Only the governor was defective. Aamco employees, however, tore down the transmission, declared it "burned up" and rebuilt it at a charge of $189.17. Subsequent examination of the transmission by a mechanic hired by the state revealed that some of the "new" parts listed on the bill were in fact the old parts which had been marked. Only two of the old marked parts reportedly had been replaced: the defective governor and a front seal valued at $2.25.

In 1970 the FTC issued a cease and desist order prohibiting Aamco from using eighteen deceptive practices including lo-balling. States still report, however, that lo-balling among other local transmission companies is widespread.

There are fads in frauds as in other areas of life. One of the most vicious is chain-referral selling, which has recently been modified to incorporate pyramid distributorships, in which a person buys a distributorship from a company for say, $5000; he then sells lesser distributorships for $2500 and supposedly gets an override on business all of them do. In fact, it doesn't work that way. The company often goes defunct, leaving only the officers richer.

In its pure form chain-referral selling leads customers to believe that by referring the names of acquaintances as prospective customers, they will have to pay nothing for a piece of merchandise, and very often will make money. For each friend who is sold, or who agrees to participate in the "advertising compaign," as it is invariably called, the victim is promised a commission. Salesmen frequently erase customers' doubts by telling them that 80 percent of those referred actually "participate" as proved by past experience. In truth, postal inspectors, by painstakingly searching through company records, have discovered that only about 5 percent of the referred actually sign up. And of course once they have sold the original customer, some companies don't bother to follow up the leads supplied, or to remit the commission if a referred friend does buy. This deceit is all the more cruel for it is being practiced on elderly people who find the lure of making a few pennies to augment their meager income irresistible.

One could produce hundreds of cases of companies perpetrating this fraud, but an especially reprehensible example was recently seen in Oklahoma City. Of this firm's activities, an investigating postal inspector, usually unemotionally objective in his reports, was moved to remark: "The viciousness of referral selling has probably never been more dramatically portrayed." He went on to write in a final report: "The operators through their well-schooled, high-pressure salesmen imported from faraway points, induced more than 1,000 financially distressed persons in Oklahoma to sign purchase contracts and promissory notes for the purchase of major household appliances, including food freezers, refrigerators, kitchen cooking ranges, stereos, television receivers, and washing machines. Each item was sold at the grossly inflated price of $660.96 on a three-year payment contract, despite the fact that identical items could at that time have been bought in numerous retail stores in Oklahoma for less than $300 each, and some for less than $250."

Particularly saddening was the experience of one man who had recently lost his left hand in an accident and could no longer work at the trade he had practiced for years. "He was burdened by medical bills, and had just taken a job at Goodwill Industries for $1 an hour," wrote the inspector, "when he received a neatly printed note in facsimile script signed by an acquaintance. It said:

> Hi,
> In a few days, at our request,
> a friend of ours will call you for
> an appointment to explain the details

of a *fabulous profit sharing program*.
You will be paid $500 for the few minutes
you devote to looking into this plan.
Since you are not obligated, hear this
out and make your own decision.
Sincerely,

"After receiving the note, he got a telephone call from the company setting up an appointment for the 'friend' to call on him and his wife. With a printed chart, the salesman showed how he could make as much as $900 in three months time, by referring names of his acquaintances to the company and signing little introductory notes the company would obligingly mail to persons whose names he furnished.

"The victim explained his dire financial circumstances, that he couldn't afford to pay for anything. The salesman assured him it was an 'advertising program' and was a means to pay all his medical bills. He was then shown the company's 'Advertising Commission Warranty.' The victim said he had no need for the appliances 'advertised' by the company, but the salesman said he had to sign up for one appliance in order to enter the program. The salesman was so convincing that the man believed the program would relieve his financial distress and he signed the papers to enter the program. The next day a stereophonic record player was delivered to his home and about a week later he received notice from a finance company that they had purchased his installment contract and that his monthly payments should be made promptly each month to them for the next three years."

This poor man sent twenty-six names to the company, but never received a single dollar in return. He is now burdened with an unwanted stereo and finance payments that put him more deeply and hopelessly in debt.

The company, operated by four persons, three from one family, cost the public an estimated $500,000 loss although it operated less than one year. Toward the end of the company's short life, its two sales offices in Oklahoma City and Tulsa were stuffed with thousands of unopened referral forms mailed in by numerous victims.

An interesting postscript to the case is that the officers of the company were arrested for mail fraud, but only the sales manager was found guilty. The other three, including the president and the vice-president, were subsequently declared innocent in a retrial. This points up how difficult it is to get a criminal conviction for consumer fraud, and thus how inappropriate our traditional criminal remedies are in stopping consumer deception. For it must be proved under the criminal fraud statutes that the scheme not only deceived consumers, but that the seller also consciously and deliberately set out to deceive. No matter how distasteful the scheme nor how many hundreds of consumers were cheated, if the jury doubts that the perpetrators sincerely *intended* to defraud, then they must find the defendants not guilty. The defendants in this case claimed that, although they may have been misguided, they actually believed that the scheme would work and carried it out in all good faith.

In granting a new trial on appeal (the verdict was guilty in the first trial), the appellate judge outlined the criteria by which the jury must come to a verdict by quoting a previous decision from the 10th circuit:

"It matters not how visionary you may find the enterprise to be, or how unreasonable the prospects of success . . . if the defendants actually believed in them. Promises made in good faith, whether they be glittering or attractive or not, are not criminal. If you believe . . . that the representations made by the defendants . . . although glittering, attractive, persuasive, and alluring, were made in good faith and not as a part of a deliberate plan to scheme or defraud or to obtain money by false pretenses, then it is your duty to find the defendants not guilty. . . ."

Being convicted of a criminal act is surely a grave matter, and I certainly would not suggest that we change the criteria for determining such convictions. No man should be branded a criminal and fined or imprisoned who has not been proved guilty of bad faith or intent to commit a wrongdoing. But the real question in protecting consumers is not whether a person who carried on such a scheme *intended* to defraud and therefore is a criminal. The pertinent question is: Should the law allow a vast number of the public to be seduced into misery—have their money stolen and their lives demeaned—by the actions of *any* soul—guided or misguided, bad-intentioned or good-intentioned? Whether such a person *intended* to deceive is quite irrelevant, if in fact he *did* deceive and is allowed to continue to deceive. In some instances of consumer fraud, criminal prosecutions are warranted. But by depending excessively on laws that punish the seller rather than stop the practice, we have yet to catch up with the realities of consumer protection.

Another pernicious type of selling which is sweeping the country is the "free gimmick," invariably accompanied by innumerable misrepresentations. It is doubtful that any American of any economic class is untouched by this scheme. A lawyer in New York whose wife was tricked into subscribing to three children's magazines under the impression that it was a "service" from the Board of Education recently wrote: "If wives of persons who are supposedly above average in education, sophistication, etc., and especially the wife of an attorney, can be so easily taken in, you can imagine what this person (a door-to-door saleswoman) must be able to do with less sophisticated persons."

The sales pitches are familiar: "This lovely *x*-cubic-foot freezer is yours absolutely free if you subscribe to our food-freezer plan." The food is usually low quality, overpriced, and the freezer is hardly free. The cost of the food more than covers the retail price of the freezer.

"Congratulations! You have just won second prize in our drawing for a vacuum cleaner, which entitles you to $150 off the purchase price." It turns out that after the $150 is subtracted from the phony $289 "regular" price, the cost is $139 which is still overpriced. The same giveaway principle is widely used in peddling sewing machines: "You have *won* a free sewing machine; the only charge to you is the price of the cabinet." The $59 "cabinet price," in truth, covers the cost of the machine and gives the seller his usual profit.

The variety is endless: "Your telephone number has been chosen for this free gift. . . ." "We want to give you five dancing lessons absolutely free if you can answer this question: Adam and Eve had two sons. One was Cain and the other was ——?" (One perverse man answered Aaron, but after the telephone solicitor recovered, she allowed that his answer was close enough—they both started with A.)

Unfortunately, another area in which the giveaway is becoming increasingly prevalent is in "educational materials," encyclopedias, magazines, and other books. In 1970, magazine subscription was at the top of the Better Business Bureau's complaints list. That year the BBB processed about 170,000 "instances of services" concerning magazines.

A magazine salesman of fifteen years experience, who finally quit the business, afterwards came to my office, anxious to make known the deplorable tactics being used in some magazine selling. He told how the sympathy "college kid gag" had given way to the something-for-nothing pitch. "Pretending you're a college kid trying to win points for a scholarship is still used in some places," he said, "but the biggest thing these days is the free-postage pitch. We tell people they get the magazine free if they will only pay the 42 cents a week postage. And they really believe it! I know some salesmen making $20,000 a year this way. Using this pitch myself I have sold $99 worth of magazines to people who are blind, who don't have shoes for their kids or a stitch of carpet on the floor. It's a rotten business, and I'm sorry I stayed in it as long as I did."

Certainly not all magazines are sold this way, and it is unfortunate that a handful of offenders are marring the reputation of the ethical dealers and publishers. The same can be said for encyclopedias, although it can also be said that many famous-name encyclopedias from supposedly reputable companies are sold by deceptive salesmanship. Consistently, the FTC has warned and brought complaints against companies that misrepresent their sets of encyclopedias as being free, an advertising promotion gift, if the customer will only pay to keep it up-to-date. In July 1967, my staff and I asked William Hesse, a graduate student at the University of Washington, and one of the Congressional interns in my office, to discover whether a newly established encyclopedia sales office in Washington, D. C., was engaging in deceptive selling by pretending to give away free sets. Hesse answered an ad promising $550 per month guaranteed salary for doing "advertising and promotion," and was put into training.

The sales pitch turned out to be laden with falsifications. Hesse was repeatedly warned never to admit he was a salesman, but to say he was "with the Promotional Division of E. E. (Educational Enterprises, Inc.) and only seeking "testimonial advertising" for the "first Major International Reference Library," whose first major sales campaign was to get under way in 1968.

Door opener (to wife only): "Hi there, I have to see your *husband*" (say it like you know him).

Door opener (to husband only): "Hi there, I have to see you for a minute!" (say it like you made a special trip just to see him; give him your name and shake his hand).

"The reason we call in the evening like this is because we have to talk to the man of the house and the wife together. OK? (*Smile*) "I'm not a salesman so please don't be alarmed. I've been asked to interview some of the families in this area . . . You know what testimonial advertising is, don't you? Well . . . Educational Enterprises has finally gone into testimonial advertising. The families that we are interviewing right now, families like yourselves, that are helping us out, we are paying them very handsomely for their help, not in cash but in the form of merchandise."

After showing them a sample of the "beautiful library," he gets to the heart of the lie, as outlined in the long, memorized speech: "That's right, you would receive this beautiful $489 masterpiece, all twenty volumes within the next two weeks, postage prepaid, as an advertising premium in exchange for your promise to write us a testimonial letter and signing the Owner's Register Card which gives us permission to use your name as a registered owner of the National Encyclopedia." Later in the canned pitch comes the catch: "Gee, I almost forgot. There is one thing I have to make crystal clear to you. We give you the Cadillac so to speak, but we have to draw the line somewhere. We don't give you the Gas and Oil. In other words, you get this complete library within two weeks, but we don't keep it up-to-date for you, too."

The salesman makes it clear they wouldn't want to place a set in the home of an "insincere" person who wouldn't "appreciate" it. There are only two things expected to show appreciation, he explains.

". . . the yearbook service that comes out each year, that adds onto your set, that keeps it up-to-date. Well, we don't give these to you or anyone. You can understand this I'm sure." Farther on, "See these coupons here?

"We have at present over 2,000 experts in every field working in our Library Research Department in New York City. Anytime something new comes up and you want to know more about it right now, all you would have to do is clip out one of these research coupons and send in a letter with the coupon to our Research Department in New York."

It turns out that the "yearbooks" are priced at $15 each for ten years. The "research coupons" cost $5 apiece, and the customer must buy ten coupons each year for ten years. All of this adds up to $650, but somehow because of "mass production," the company has been able to cut the cost to $335.50—just 9 cents a day. The salesman gives the customer a calendar bank in which to deposit his daily dime, and attempts to persuade him to pay it all off in two years instead of ten.

The pitch is peppered throughout with insincerities and lies. On the contract there is no mention of a "free" encyclopedia. The salesman is instructed to write "20 volume encyclopedia" and the price. All of the other is verbal misrepresentation, which is difficult to prove in court. Such words are not binding, but the customer's signature on the contract is.

Aside from harm to the customer, it seems to me reprehensible that grown men are hiring young boys and teaching them to lie with such cynicism and contemptuousness. For many of these young men, it is their first introduction to the world of business. The better-educated boys who already have a career planned may come away with a bad taste for business in general. (There were fifteen boys in Hesse's class and how many stayed with it, we don't know. Hesse left after three days and reported several boys had already confessed to him that they didn't "have the stomach for it.")

Other boys may find their lies so successful they make such selling a way of life. The reformed magazine salesman who came to my office said his career started when he took a temporary selling job, pretending he was working his way through college. He intended to stay only three months, but found it so lucrative, he stayed fifteen years. He admitted his conscience bothered him in the beginning, but "I got so wound up in making that sale, I got so I didn't notice it."

Perhaps no sales pitch has been around longer than the "fearsell." Even the rulers of ancient countries were intimidated into buying amulets lest their souls be damned or they suffer a dreadful accident. In today's sophisticated marketplace, peddlers still make fortunes preying on people's fears. One woman wrote me she had four perfectly healthy maple trees felled by a wandering "tree surgeon," who told her they were rotten and could come crashing down on her house. Gangs of salesmen, according to the National Fire Protection Association, are scouring the country, displaying gruesome photographs of families burned to death in home fires. Their object is to sell home fire-alarm systems which are invariably outrageously priced and sometimes worthless.

Every spring, as regularly as the rain, reports the BBB, the phony chimney repairmen show up. They knock off a few bricks and claim the chimney is about to topple, or claim it is clogged and that the whole family is in imminent danger of dying from carbon monoxide poisoning. Some termite inspectors carry bugs which they plant in the wood, and then inform the alarmed homeowner that unless the "termites" are exterminated, the house will quickly deteriorate. Often the salesmen pose as government inspectors. That they extort millions of dollars from frightened Americans is well-documented.

A classic case is that of the Holland Furnace Company, which for thirty years conducted what Consumers Union branded "one of the most pernicious sales rackets in the country." Holland Furnace, based in Holland, Michigan, with 500 offices throughout the country and 5,000 employees, was the leading furnace-replacement firm in the nation. Through its "tear down and scare tactics" it victimized hundreds of thousands of Americans. Misrepresenting themselves as "furnace engineers" and "safety inspectors," the salesmen frequently dismantled a furnace, condemned it as hazardous and refused to re-assemble it, stating they didn't want to be "accessories to murder." The salesmen were merciless. In New England, branch salesmen from one office sold an elderly infirm woman nine new furnaces in six years, for a total take of $18,000.

One woman in San Francisco became suspicious after a Holland Furnace salesman condemned her furnace. She called the Better Business Bureau, which dispatched both an inspector from the local Pacific Gas and Electric Company and a Better Business Bureau representative with a tape recorder. The gas inspector pronounced the furnace perfectly safe and in good repair. When the salesman returned to clinch the sale, he unknowingly delivered his pitch both to the woman and into a hidden tape recorder. It went this way:

". . . the flue pipe instead of taking all of the smoke and fumes up the flue, a good percentage of them are going up in the house. . . . See where she's burnt out over there . . . that's going right up into your house. . . . The warm air plenum is above here, which means that the smoke and fumes go up in here, and then that fan turns on back there. . . . I'm not saying this to scare you, I'm just saying it to impress you. . . . This is worse than the raw gas, because the raw gas you can smell. This is carbon monoxide. . . . This is no different than if you took the exhaust pipe from your automobile and ran it in here. . . . I would actually be doing you a favor . . . by shutting your furnace off. . . I'm not doing that to sell you a furnace, I'm just trying to be honest with you. . . . It's not healthy. I would replace it and I would do it now. . . . It's leaking. . . . We can allow you $28.50 as junk for that old furnace."

The amazing thing about this fraud, besides the boldness of the company and the size of its loot, is its longevity, which once again painfully illustrates the inefficacy of our present laws to bring deceptive practices to a quick halt. Although victims began complaining about Holland Furnace in the 1930s and the FTC soon after began collecting proof, which is now voluminous, it was not until January 1965 that the company finally was forced to close its doors. The ex-president of the company was sentenced to six months in prison (the first time an official of a major corporation has been held criminally responsible for the misrepresentations of its salesmen), and the corporation was fined $100,000 for violation of a court injunction issued in 1959. The fine reportedly was sufficient to cause bankruptcy. In the meantime, Holland Furnace at the height of its business cost the American public 30 million dollars a year.

If one were writing a textbook on deceptive selling, these five schemes—phony special price, bait and switch, referral selling, the free gimmick, and the fear-sell—could be described as the basics of the course. For with a little ingenuity they can be, and are being, applied to the shady salesmanship of any product imaginable, from pots and pans to real estate. The five schemes are used alone or in endless combination with one another and with dozens of other misrepresentations, such as "I'm from the school board to test your child's musical talent"; "Of course you can cancel the contract if you change your mind"; "I'm a veteran just back from Vietnam"; "Our carpeting is cheaper because it is sold in 'factory units'" (a factory unit turns out to be one-third of a yard). "If you don't want the free magazines yourself, we are authorized to donate them for you to the local school; they say they *need* these magazines." "I see that your vacuum sweeper (sewing machine, automobile, washing machine) is completely shot." "You're only signing a receipt," when, in fact, it is a sales contract or promissory note.

In addition to these five basic schemes there are several hundred others. Among the most prevalent, pernicious, and costly are:

Charity swindles for nonexistent churches, hospitals, veterans' organizations, and so on. This scheme accounts for a 100 million dollar a year loss to the public.

Business opportunity rackets. A person seeking extra income is induced to buy an expensive vending machine with the promise that he can install the machine in a local place of business and collect the proceeds; or a piece of equipment such as a floor polisher with the promise that floor-polishing jobs will be referred to him by the seller. Victims invariably discover that no place of business will take the vending machine and that no jobs are forthcoming.

Phony home improvements. These swindlers are often fly-by-nights who insist on cash immediately, and for good reason. Their lightning rod "cables" turn out to be silver-painted rope; they resurface driveways by covering them with motor oil; they neglect to mention that when they "paint" a house, they don't use waterproof paint, and with the first rain the paint washes off. For more than thirty years one Irish family known as the "Terrible Williamsons" has worked the country performing phony house-repair jobs. It is said that the clan on the road now numbers at least one hundred.

Substandard correspondence and vocational schools. Undoubtedly this is one of the most disheartening rackets of all, for it preys on the aspirations of the elderly and undereducated who are falsely led to believe they can raise their station in life by subscribing to one of these costly substandard courses. The courses purport to teach such occupational skills as motel management, insurance claim adjusting, data processing, telegraphy, how to pass a civil service examination, and how to operate a bulldozer (without ever seeing one). After spending hundreds, sometimes thousands, of dollars on this shabby education, the "graduate" finds that when he goes out to seek a job, he is totally unqualified and no one will hire him.

Land-fraud sales. Thousands of persons, many seeking retirement homes or investments, have bought lots, sight unseen, on the basis of glowing brochures or color slides that bore no resemblance to the actual land site. Some of the "developments" were never developed at all and turned out to be in the swamps, in the desert, on the tops of mountains, under water, and even in the jungles and lava beds of South America.

Why are we unable to control such deceptive practices and to prevent consumer exploitation? Primarily because our present laws are outmoded and inadequate to deal with the modern complexities of consumer fraud. Most of our laws on dishonest selling were designed long ago to catch and punish a few "hardened criminals" and not to cope with the vast web of subtle deceits and credit merchandising abuses that characterizes the businesses of today's "soft-sell" swindlers. Generally, our legal remedies have two defects: they are ineffective in halting deceptive selling, and they make virtually no provisions for redressing the wrong, whether by freeing the cheated consumer of a fraudulently induced debt or by reimbursing him.

The Federal Trade Commission, as the federal agency primarily responsible for stopping deceptive selling on a national scale, has broad powers and has been effective in curtailing unscrupulous sellers in interstate commerce for half a century. Nevertheless, we cannot depend on the FTC alone to halt all deceptive selling nation-wide. Even with an addition in personnel, it would still be impossible for the FTC to stop all deceptive selling even within its interstate jurisdiction. And the FTC also has certain limitations in its powers to protect consumers.

As we have seen, the FTC cannot stop deceptive selling operations that limit their activities to intrastate commerce, staying within a state's borders, which is where most such selling occurs. Nor can the FTC in some cases move fast enough to halt the swindlers before they have victimized a number of consumers and accumulated a small fortune. Nor can the FTC act on behalf of an individual con-sumer; it can move only when a substantial number of Americans have been injured (enough to make an FTC action "in the public interest").

Then too, the FTC can only compel the offender to stop working his deceptive arts on future customers; it cannot order him to reim-burse those whom he has already cheated or to cancel collection of their debts.

At the state level, officials who attempt to protect consumers are incredibly handicapped by inadequate laws. Although many states have recently passed effective laws and set up machinery to enforce them, the picture of state consumer legislation is, as a whole, dreary indeed. An informal survey by the FTC in June 1971 showed that only thirty-two states could be said to have "good" or "excellent" laws prohibiting deceptive selling practices. At least one-third of the states have pitifully weak laws. Effective consumer legislation is especially lacking in Alabama, Georgia, Kentucky, Louisiana, Mis-sissippi, Montana, Nebraska, Nevada, Ohio, Oklahoma, Tennessee, Utah, West Virginia, and Wyoming.

In a few states legislation is simply nonexistent. Only a handful of states regulate correspondence schools, fraudulent selling of land, or specifically outlaw bait advertising.

Absence of laws, however, is not the only problem in the states. For as the *Columbia Law Review* has noted, "The states have adopted a staggering number of statutes noteworthy for their ad hoc and piecemeal approach to the problems of advertising control and for the very slight degree to which they are enforced." In truth, all but three states—Arkansas, Delaware, and New Mexico—have a "Printer's Ink" statute (named for the advertising magazine of the same name) making it a misdemeanor to make an "untrue, deceptive, or misleading" statement with the intent to sell a product.

One would think this law so comprehensive that it would virtually wipe out deceptive advertising in the states. Such is not the case, for the law, broad as it is, contains an insurmountable flaw; it is a *criminal* statute, as are many of the other measures adopted by the states to halt deceptive selling. Under the criminal statute, conviction demands proof beyond a reasonable doubt, and carries with it fines, possible jail sentences, and the stigma of being branded a criminal.

Since its adoption in 1911, the Printer's Ink statute may have deterred some sellers from deceptive practices, but the number of culprits it has actually brought to justice is infinitesimal. Law enforcement officials overwhelmingly consider the law so unrealistic that they don't attempt to enforce it. A survey by the *Columbia Law Review* in 1956 discovered that during nearly fifty years, only "a handful of prosecutions" had been brought under the Printer's Ink statutes throughout the country. Many attorneys general and county prosecutors freely admitted that they had never tried to enforce it. One reason is that local prosecutors are burdened with trying to halt major felonies such as murder, rape, and robbery, and are disinclined to waste their time on such a relatively small "crime" as false advertising or selling. Another reason is that few prosecutors believe they will get a conviction. They have found that juries are hesitant to find a man guilty of a crime for what may merely be "overzealous salesmanship"; consequently, few public officials prosecute.

Two law students at the University of Pennsylvania, investigating the ineffectiveness of consumer legislation, found that "even when a law enforcement official believes that a particular scheme has been made actionable by statute, he often does not prosecute because of a widely held belief that, except in the most egregious circumstances, fraudulent operators should not be treated like criminals. Lawyers, business leaders, and prosecutors have stated that 'judges, juries, and district attorneys do not like to put businessmen in jail.' One district attorney, when asked by the attorney general to prosecute an alleged fraudulent operator, retorted: 'I can't even get a conviction when they stick a gun in somebody's back; how can I get one when they just talk him out of his money?' "

Trying to control consumer fraud completely by proving criminality is an outmoded concept. But even if the criminal statutes could be enforced (and New York, for example, has achieved rare success in obtaining convictions), it is doubtful that society's purpose is best served by only putting a swindler behind bars. The sentence is usually short (in Pennsylvania one man who made $300,000 selling fake automobile parts was sentenced to a term of one year), after which the wrongdoer is set free to spend his ill-gotten money, and the cheated consumer, who understandably wants no justice so much as his money back, is left to suffer without restitution.

Additionally, the hit-and-miss proposition of locking up criminals who defraud the public is inefficient in halting consumer fraud on a broad scale. Only one operator can be put out of business at a time, after long, costly court proceedings, while thousands of other gypsters—perhaps associated with the same company or swindle— are allowed to flourish. And even after a short prison term, the ex-convict can start up a new racket, using the same fraudulent techniques, and rob Americans of a fortune, while local authorities once again gear up their machinery to start the slow, painful process of gathering evidence against him on the new charge.

The injured consumer can bring suit himself, but few do. They soon discover that lawyer's fees, court costs, and time away from employment will cost more than they can possibly recover. A woman in Ohio, who hired an attorney to keep from losing her $15,000 house because of a home-improvement repairs bill of $7,200, had already paid a legal fee of $1,500 and still did not receive her house back. Under strict legal requirements in most states, the complainant must have an exceptionally good case in order to win; many times it is only his word against that of the shady seller.

Invariably, the victim has also unknowingly, by signing the contract, given away a number of rights of defense and agreed that nothing the seller told him, unless specifically stated in the contract, is binding. When a group of lawyers in Pennsylvania were asked in an informal survey what they would do with a client who had been gypped out of several hundred dollars for carpeting in a "bait and switch" scheme, they unanimously agreed: "Send him home."

Clearly, the weak, inappropriate, poorly enforced, hit-and-miss legislation that is the rule throughout the nation is quite undependable in combating the complexities and size of our present-day consumer deception. In this antiquated system of justice, the dishonest steal quietly off to count their loot, while the injured consumer is sacrificed on the altar of legislative short-sightedness.

Chapter 2

Shame in the Ghettos

When the law lags behind the needs of society, we can expect some ugly consequences. And in the area of consumer protection, the evils of allowing legalized thievery to flourish are nowhere more strikingly evident than among the poor, especially the minority groups in the ghettos. The exploitation of these people by unscrupulous local merchants and fly-by-night operators is one of the silent shames of our country.

From coast to coast, mainly in our urban areas, those who can least afford to pay are paying unconscionable prices for junk, pawned off on them through trickery, deceit, and fraud. By signing contracts containing the most inhumane clauses, these poor people legally bind themselves into misery. And when they cannot pay or refuse to pay, they find themselves pushed even further into destitution by a legal system which is incomprehensible to them and which has become perverted from a device for protecting the innocent to a means of abetting the dishonest. Although this is a strong indictment, it is not exaggerated. It is no more than what anyone who has worked in the ghettos or studied these problems will confirm.

In broad perspective, many of the abuses inflicted on the poor, especially in regard to installment contracts, are used to exploit the middle class as well as the poor. But it is in the poverty-stricken areas, where the people are least able to get "good" credit and are the most vulnerable to the persuasions of the prevaricators, that the ugliest manifestations are found.

The plight of the poverty-stricken consumer is all the more poignant when it is realized that his pursuit of goods and credit, which in turn makes him so vulnerable to callous exploitation, is in reality what has been called "compensatory consumption," a desire to infuse his existence with dignity denied him elsewhere by accumulating material goods. An excellent description of the poor's situation is given by former FTC Commissioner Mary Gardiner Jones:

"Our poverty-stricken citizens . . . are either on welfare, or hold down the most menial jobs which bring them a pitifully inadequate income and certainly no dignity or sense of pride in themselves or in the job which they are doing. They spend almost 60 percent of their incomes on food and rent alone. They are always in debt, live only on the threshold of a bare subsistence in dismal slums haunted by insecurity and fear and dominated by the constant threat of slipping even further down in the economic and social hierarchy. . . . Yet they are constantly surrounded and reminded of all the material benefits of our great society which are enjoyed by everyone else. . . . Like us they are the recipients of the daily advertising messages of the necessities of life which we should buy, of the constant urgings to buy now and pay later, of the glowing promises of no money down or low weekly payments. The social pressure on them to consume is almost irresistible, not simply because of their actual physical needs for many of these possessions, but also because of their deep psychological needs for self-respect, for dignity, for a feeling of belonging, and for approval from their neighbors. . . . The only sense of status which is in any way available to them is through possession of the material accoutrements of our economy . . . an automobile, a sewing machine, a television set or a combination console, radio-phonograph. . . ."

Thus, to satisfy deep human needs, the poor are driven into what David Caplovitz, a sociology professor at Columbia University and author of *The Poor Pay More,* a classic study of the problems of the poor in New York City, has described as a "commercial jungle in which exploitation and fraud are the norm rather than the exception."

It has been well-documented by Professor Caplovitz and others that the poor, who can least afford to have their earning power diminished by high prices, pay dearly for merchandise available much cheaper to the middle class. The poor are at the mercy of high-priced neighborhood stores and door-to-door salesmen. Professor Caplovitz found that in New York City those with family incomes of under $3,500 consistently paid more for appliances than those earning over $3,500. For example, 46 percent of the lower income group paid more than $300 for a table model television; only 37 percent of the higher income group paid such a high price. Similarly, 49 percent of those with the under $3,500 income paid more than $230 for a washing machine; only 35 percent of those earning over $3,500 paid a comparable price.

A comparative shopping study, made by the Mobilization for Youth in New York City, showed that an Admiral 19-inch-screen portable television set cost from $179 to $200 cash on the Lower East Side. An identical set was sold in a major downtown discount house for $139. Three women shoppers in the same survey also demonstrated how costly the color of your skin can be. They each priced the same television set in a Lower East Side store. The quoted price to a young, white law student was $125, to a Puerto Rican housewife, $139, and to a Black housewife, $200—a racial price differential of 60 percent! Shopping surveys in Boston, Philadelphia, Chicago, and San Francisco reveal the same pattern: the poor are paying exorbitant prices, usually 75 to 100 percent more for goods from stores in low-income areas as compared with those in "ethical" stores patronized by the middle class.

With pathetic regularity, the merchandise bought by the poor is shoddy, and they are deceived into buying it. Professor Caplovitz reports the frustration of a middle-aged Black mother on welfare, who unknowingly responded to a bait ad promising the reupholstery of a couch for $49.95.

"I phoned them and they sent out a salesman. I asked him to show me the material. He pulled out some patterns and looked at them and said, 'These aren't so hot. I really want to give customers something they'll be satisfied with.' Then he flipped to the higher-priced patterns—but I didn't know they were higher priced then. I picked out a pattern and asked him how much. He told me $149. But I only had $49 in cash and wanted to pay only in cash, so I told him that this was too high. He praised the material so much, talking about its quality and durability, that I finally told him that if I could get an account I'd take it. He gave me a contract. I just took a quick look and signed it. They sent for the couch and returned it two weeks later. The work on the seams of the pillows was awful. . . . Six months later, the wire in the springs popped out the side."

Countless poor people are deceived into buying second-hand merchandise, believing it to be new. An elderly lady in Washington, D. C., rather wistfully tells how she was tricked into buying a 19-inch used television for $355 by signing a "receipt." In response to a radio-spot commercial that ironically began: "Empire Furniture and Appliance Company has sold thousands of television sets to people just like you because Empire gives you a TV deal that's unbeatable," the woman called and asked for the company's "free home demonstration—no obligation."

"When the TV was delivered," she said, "I told the driver the set was dirty, but he said it was only dust and can be wiped off. I paid him $25 and he gave me a receipt. . . . He rushed out very fast and I do not have good light in my room. So it was not before daytime next day that I noticed I got an old set and not a new set as ordered. . . . I never knowingly signed a contract and never received a copy of a contract. I only meant to have signed on the clipboard of the delivery man that I received the set. . . . I am not so good in reading and writing and I do not understand words and meanings which are in a sales contract. I would never have signed a contract of any kind without my son or daughter present to read it for me." Yet this poor elderly woman had without her knowledge signed a contract, agreeing to pay $13.75 in twenty-four monthly payments for the old set.

An appliance store in Maryland, according to reports, consistently sells repossessed television sets for as high as $450, after paying only $25 to $50 for them. A prospective customer, enticed by advertising, such as "No down-payment, have TV in your home *tonight!*" enters the store and is disappointed to find only rows of beat-up old sets. The salesman assures him, however, that the advertised new sets haven't come in yet, but that by signing a contract "ordering" a new set, he can take one of the old sets home to use in the meantime. What the customer actually signs is a conditional sales contract, purchasing the old repossessed set at an exorbitant price. The new sets, of course, never arrive. The contract is sold to a finance company, and according to law, the purchaser must make his payments.

Washington, D. C., like other major cities, has a "mercantile row" which caters to low-income groups. Here in this area—Seventh Street in the District of Columbia—one merchant does a thriving business in watches, rings, radios, television sets, eyeglasses, and small appliances by selling the prestige of having credit. Salesmen are dispatched onto the sidewalk to detain passersby and entice them into the store by offering them a free gift and a "credit card." One elderly man told how he was approached by a sales clerk who said: "Would you like to come in and get this gift?" He was handed two cards. One read: "FREE GIFT for YOU! No obligation. Don't buy a thing. Don't spend a Minute. Just present this card and Get your FREE GIFT." The other read: "Certifies that Bearer is an AAA-1 Preferred Customer. Instant Credit. No Money Down. Make your own Terms. This card certifies that you have a preferred credit rating and attests to your character excellence."

"Well, you don't know what kind of gift it is until you go inside for curiosity," said the man. So he did and was disappointed to discover he was given only a ball-point pen. But bewildered by the attention and flattered by the offer of credit (he had never been given credit at any store), he did not want to pass it up. He was talked into "opening an account" by signing a conditional sales contract for a watch. His confusion over the purchase (he was "kind of scared because I never had an account before I got this account") is typical of the lack of sophistication of such low-income consumers.

Question by an FTC attorney: Could you tell us, do you remember, Mr. White, when you signed this document?

Answer: Well, I signed it right after I got the account with them, after I realized they wanted me to open an account.

Q: Did they tell you what this document was, Mr. White?

A: You mean before I signed this?

Q: Before you signed it or after you signed it. Were you aware of what you were signing?

A: Well, I knew a little about how to open an account. As far as signing this contract, they told me to sign a contract and I signed. . . .

Q: (Holding the contract): Can you tell me what this is?

A: This is the contract here.

Q: What is the contract for? Do you know what it is for?

A: It is for when you open an account. You have to buy it.

For the privilege of having credit, Mr. White, a Negro earning $60 a week in a government cafeteria, paid $86 for a cheap watch worth one-tenth that much and paid it off at $2.50 a week. This store attaches price tags to its merchandise, but what customers don't know is that this amount hardly represents the item's true value; 90 percent of the price is markup. The store sells transistor radios for $59.50 which the store buys wholesale at $3.45 each. Toasters are marked up from $5.49 to $49.50, and sets of aluminum cookware from $6.47 to $69.50—in all cases at least a 1,000 percent markup for the "easy credit."

Another shoddy practice of one Seventh Street merchant, according to several reports, is to offer free eye examinations, obviously designed to sell extravagantly priced glasses even to those who don't need them. The store sends out a mailing, inviting people in for a "free eye examination, no obligation." A sign in the store also announces: "Have Your EYES Examined Free; Doctor in the House." Several people have sworn that after the examination, although they insisted they didn't want the glasses, the lenses were quickly inserted into frames and handed to them before they could leave the store. When they refused to buy them, they were intimidated into signing sales contracts for the glasses with "You *have* to buy them; we made them especially to fit *you;* we can't sell them to anyone else." When one woman so treated complained to a clerk that her vision through one of the lenses was blurry, the clerk replied: "You'll get used to it." Although a pair of glasses was advertised at a discount of "from $7.50 complete," glasses often sold for $59.50 and $79.50, more than twice what other optometrists in Washington charge.

A mother of five children said she was lured into the store by a direct mailing piece. "My eyes weren't bothering me," she said, "but I wanted to be on the safe side. . . . I was given a rain scarf as my free gift, and was introduced to a man in a white coat who was called Doctor. . . . This man examined my eyes and told me I needed glasses. He said that sunlight would cause me to have eye strain and that I needed sunglasses. Additionally he said I needed glasses for reading. I had both pairs of glasses made up for me and I signed a contract to pay for them at $59.50 per pair plus carrying charges of $21.42." The prevailing retail price for such glasses was $32; her glasses were practically zero prescription (Rx .25 cyl, the weakest prescription possible next to plain glass), and an optometrist who retested her vision confirmed that although wearing the glasses would not be harmful, it was quite "dubious" that she needed them at all.

This woman worked at a drugstore as a countergirl and was the sole support of herself and five children; she earned $85 every two weeks. Yet $20 monthly, 12 percent of this bare subsistence income, was diverted from the necessities of food and clothing to pay for the unnecessary glasses. Thus—and this is a fact too often ignored—such practices not only exploit poverty, they actually *create* poverty. After witnessing the hardships caused by this one store alone, an investigating attorney for the FTC wrote: "The business methods are so incredible and effect such fraud and deception on that element of the consuming public that he regularly deals with that it is almost impossible to describe them."

Perhaps the most striking revelation to me after reviewing the FTC poverty cases was how skillfully these unscrupulous salesmen prey on the fears and insecurities of the poor, and how susceptible the poor are to such blandishments and threats. Decidedly, those who specialize in selling to the poor are astute students of the psychological and sociological implications of what it means to be impoverished in today's affluent society. These so-called businessmen shamelessly exploit the poor man's desire for credit, his longing for respect, his fear of losing his job, his home—what little security he has built up—and most of all, his fear of being doomed to eternal poverty. In one of the most vicious rackets I'm sure has ever been worked anywhere, a company in the District of Columbia in 1966, under the guise of operating an urban renewal project, frightened countless ghetto residents into signing contracts for aluminum fronts for their houses, at prices as high as $4,000 and $5,000. The salesmen implied that if they did not "urban-renew," they would be "urban-removed."

Many salesmen—both in stores and door-to-door—contemptuously intersperse their sales pitches with "Mister" and insist, "Just call me by my first name." One home-improvement company working the Black ghettos in Washington, D. C., pointedly used all-white work crews, whom the company representative in the presence of the Black homeowner always referred to as "boys." In fact, the success of this particular scheme depended almost entirely on the salesman's skill at faking solicitude, insidiously calculated to throw the victim off guard.

It was a referral scheme, and the product was an intercom system, consisting of an AM—FM radio, master panel, six remote speakers, a fire detection and panic alarm system. The company promised to pay $335 for each fifteen names submitted and a $100 prize for each sale made as a result.

Since the financing risk was high—many of the people attracted to the scheme were not working or were on welfare and signed up in the desperate hope of making money—the intercom company sought security for the debt, namely a lien on the purchaser's property. Knowing, however, that the customers would balk at signing away such rights—after all, they didn't think they were buying something; they thought the company was paying them—ths salesmen engaged in an ingenious bit of chicanery. After the customer had signed the "participation plan" (conditional sales contract) and the intercom system was installed, a man posing as the company attorney or public relations man casually dropped by the house and made solicitious inquiries about whether the work had been properly done. He carried a checklist, which he meticulously filled in, asking whether the workmen were neat and courteous, whether the customer was genuinely pleased, and so on. Almost as an afterthought, he said: "Oh, yes, I nearly forgot. The salesman was in such a hurry that he brought you the wrong form to sign the first time." He wrote VOID in large print across the original contract and asked: "Now please sign these new papers. Just a formality." Disarmed by such unusual deferential treatment, many customers trustingly signed without reading the second document, which apparently was also folded over to conceal its contents. What they unknowingly signed was a promissory note and deed of trust on their house.

It is shameful to see these shabby homes, paint peeling, front porches crumbling, inhabited by the elderly and infirm, and yet replete with an elaborate intercom system that cost more than $1,000 and was worth approximately $200. But worse still is the feeling of desperation that besets these people when they cannot make payments and are threatened with the loss of their homes. A widow in her seventies wrote to the *Washington Star:* "In May, when I sent them $30 (instead of $38.60) so I could buy some food with the $8, the man called saying if I didn't send him the $8 he would take out a lien on my house which I didn't know he had. . . . Please help me. I am an elderly lady, a widow who got fooled."

One cannot long study the rackets aimed at the poor in the District or in any other area of the country without seeing one fact become increasingly clear: deceptive selling generally, and especially in the ghettos, is built solidly on the back of our outmoded law. The success of all manner of schemes and chicanery depends almost entirely on the swindler's assurance of easily collecting the debt through legal channels.

Some local merchants and door-to-door outfits, which use deceptive methods, pretend to make a credit check. In truth, they care little whether the customer can pay. They will burden the poor with unconscionable debts after determining one fact: can they collect legally? Does the person have property which can be legally confiscated and sold in case of default in payments? Does he have a job where his wages can be attached—in the legal term, garnisheed—that is, a certain portion deducted from each paycheck until the debt is paid? It is ironic that many merchants who exploit the poor are no longer interested in peddling merchandise for the profit of a legitimate markup. They use cheap merchandise only as a means of selling enormous credit debts which they can then forcibly extract by using our courts as their collection agencies.

Not surprisingly, the potency of garnishment as a weapon of extortion against the poor has hardly gone unnoticed by the swindlers. So widely is it used that it has given rise to a new phenomenon reported by officials in many cities: "garnishment rings" that operate principally in the ghettos. Examinations of court records in several cities show that certain firms, both dealers and finance companies, dealing exclusively with the poor, account for a suspicious number of garnishments. One merchant in Washington, D. C., selling eyeglasses, for example, filed 411 garnishment cases in court during a thirteen-month period. This was compared with only 217 filed by the District's largest department store which does hundreds of times more business.

In Cleveland, Ohio, with the help of a state legislator, local officials, and the Ohio Consumer Frauds and Crime Section of the Attorney General's Office, a garnishment racket involving several merchants and finance companies was exposed in early 1967. At least half a dozen appliance stores in Cleveland's East Side Negro section typically operated, reported Ohio's consumer fraud officials, by luring desperate people who needed instant cash. The stores enticed people to sign installment sales contracts by offering them a cash loan on the spot—most often $50, but as little as $25 or as much as $125, which was then added on to the contract in a disguised form. Such a practice—lending money without a license—is illegal in Ohio; it is also in such instances difficult to prove.

Unable to borrow money from legitimate sources, the poor, under the pressure of emergencies such as medical bills and unpaid debts, found the "instant cash" a powerful inducement to buy merchandise they did not need or want. One man admitted that one Christmas he bought two television sets, one stereophonic record player, and a tape recorder, *all in one week,* and got $25 from each merchant. He subsequently had three garnishments filed against him. Another man said he was induced to sign his name to a sales contract in return for two-fifths of whiskey.

At its worst, the scheme operated this way: a customer purchased a stove at the high price of $239; by the time finance charges, insurance, a "finder's fee" (the stores sometimes send solicitors out door-to-door to find prospects), and a conglomeration of other charges, including the well-disguised cash loan and its interest, were totaled, the price due was $818. The purchaser was given thirty days to make the first payment. If thirty days came and went and the debtor was delinquent, sometimes by only one day, the store insisted on immediate payment of the *entire* balance, which they can legally do under a clause in the contract called the "acceleration clause," reading: "In event of any default, the balance of this obligation shall at once become due and payable at the option of the holder hereof." Obviously, the poor purchaser had no means of raising such a large sum immediately, so the store then repossessed the stove.

Since the merchandise was now used, it brought at public auction perhaps $75, a sum which the store obligingly, as the law required, deducted from the purchaser's debt. Although the hapless owner now had no stove at all, he was still obligated to pay the store the remaining $743, which is known as a "deficiency judgment."

If he balked at paying off $743 for something he no longer possessed, the store had little worry. Their lawyers simply filed a garnishment proceeding in court against his wages; and his employer was required by law to deduct a certain percentage from each paycheck to meet the bad debt and forward it to the store.

Among these many incredible facts of law is another: the cheated Ohio consumer, as is true in some other states, was even deprived of the opportunity of defending himself in court against such exploitation through garnishment. Inserted in fine print into the sales contract he signed was an insidious agreement, legally called a cognovit note, commonly called a "confession of judgment" clause. By signing such a document, the customer waives his right to defend himself in a court of law. He has no chance to confront the creditor with charges of fraud or to show cause in court why his wages should not be garnisheed. The garnishment is slapped on automatically; for by signing the "confession of judgment" contract, the debtor has *pleaded guilty in advance.*

The rights he signs away are awesome, as revealed by the language in the contracts used by certain stores in Ohio: "We and each of us, jointly and severally, hereby authorize any attorney-at-law in the state of Ohio, at any time after this obligation becomes due, with or without process, to appear for us or either of us in any court of record in the state of Ohio, and confess judgment in favor of the legal holder of this note for the amount then appearing due hereon according to the terms hereof, and court costs, against us or either of us, to release all errors and the right of second trial, and the rights of error or appeal and stay of execution."

In Philadelphia, also, we can witness the struggle of the poor against the injustices of the marketplace. Pennsylvania has an unusual situation. It is one of two states that prohibit the garnishment of wages. Instead, creditors here often obtain liens on property, including homes, as security. Until very recently, when it was found unconstitutional by a federal court, the state, like a number of other states, also permitted "a confession of judgment" clause in promissory notes. That meant that any time a payment was missed, the financial institution holding the debtor's note could notify the sheriff to seize the debtor's property and put it up for auction without going through court. Now, creditors must go through court to foreclose, but Philadelphians are still losing their property for unjust debts by default judgments or strict enforcement of the notes by the court.

The following cases came to me through the Consumers Education and Protective Association (CEPA), a nonprofit organization in Philadelphia which works mainly among minority groups to educate consumers, to obtain redress of wrongs, and to achieve reforms in legislation. The group is supported by such distinguished scholars as Professor Caplovitz, and an attorney who often represents CEPA is John O. Honnold, Jr., professor of law at the University of Pennsylvania.

In September 1963, a door-to-door salesman persuaded Mr. and Mrs. John Gallman of Philadelphia, a Black couple in their sixties, to have the front of their house painted, tuckpointed and stripped, and a new storm door installed. Unknown to the Gallmans, it was a job worth perhaps $200 to $250 (their house was only fourteen feet wide), but they agreed to pay the workmen $650. Mr. Gallman cannot read or write, so he signed the papers with an X. His wife also signed the contract, noting the price as $650. At the same time, says Mr. Gallman, the salesman instructed her to sign "something else," which turned out to be a judgment note, putting up their possessions as security and containing the confession of judgment provision. Soon afterward, the Gallmans received notice from a local company, the Mid-Penn Discount Corporation that they owed not $650, but $1,632. That figure, which apparently included $982 in finance charges—or 150 percent of the actual debt—was filled in on the judgment note after she signed it, Mrs. Gallman maintains.

The tactics here are common, says Max Weiner, educational director for CEPA. He explains that salesmen trick people into signing judgment notes for outrageous amounts, sometimes several times what they think they are paying. "On the contract it says, for example, you have bought something for $650. You sign it. At the same time they present you with a blank judgment note, the salesman says, 'Sign this too.' You have just signed a contract for $650, so you assume the note is for the same amount. Sometimes customers are told they are merely signing an 'order' for the merchandise. The salesman takes back the signed note and fills in whatever amount he wants—well, not whatever he wants, for there are laws on the maximum amount of finance charges allowed—but he fills it in for the maximum figure, which in this case was $1,632—without the customer's consent or knowledge."

The Gallmans realized they had been swindled, but they didn't complain; "being quiet people," says Weiner, "they went along making the payments of $33.98 per month, which were to run for forty-eight months." About two years later, Mr. Gallman suffered an attack of asthma and was out of work. The Gallmans dropped four months behind on their payments. After Gallman recovered, they struggled to make up the payments, and during the next year and a half, they paid faithfully every month and even doubled-up twice on payments, making them only two months delinquent, or $67.96 behind. At this point the finance company had collected forty-two of the forty-eight payments—$1,427.16 of the total $1,632. The Gallmans had only $200 more to go on that ill-gotten, unconscionably high debt, when on May 22, 1967, the finance company decided it was time to close in for the old delinquent payment of $67. (Such timing is not always accidental. Attorneys for the poor across the country report that many companies wait until the debtor has substantially reduced his debt before taking legal action. That way, the company is a double-winner; it has nearly all the money owed on the contract and the man's property as well. It is true that the finance company must return any money from the sale that is in excess of the debt, but the property is hardly ever sold for what it is worth. In numerous cases, the company itself or its dummy bidders arrange to purchase the goods at a disgracefully low price. They, of course, then resell it at a higher price.)

The attorney for the Mid-Penn Discount Corporation demanded a writ of execution on the Gallmans' judgment note, and the sheriff's office, as demanded by law, put the Gallmans' property up for public auction. If the debtor resists, the sheriff's office is required to seize the possessions by force. Thus, on May 22, two sheriff's deputies and eight policemen smashed the glass in the front door and broke into the home of Mr. and Mrs. Gallman with the intent of confiscating the furniture. Mrs. Gallman, described as a "frail, elderly Negro lady," became hysterical and attempted to ward off the men with a barbecue fork. It was later claimed by a deputy sheriff that Mr. Gallman tried to defend his property by unsteadily waving an old, rusty shotgun.

But the law was not to be deterred. Mrs. Gallman, bleeding from a scuffle, was taken to the hospital. Mr. Gallman was overcome by the policemen. And not long afterward, a truck came and emptied the house. All of their furniture, accumulated during thirty-five years of marriage and valued at $2,347 was put on the auction block. It was bought by the vice-president of Mid-Penn Discount Corporation, the finance company that had ordered the auction, for the pathetic sum of $90.

Three months later, Mrs. Gallman was still hobbling around with her foot in a cast; the neighbors and a local dealer had donated some old furniture on which the Gallmans sit, mostly in silence, just waiting. For, although stripped to near-destitution and living off the charity of their friends, these poor people have still not seen an end to the bewildering workings of the law. Both Marie and John Gallman were charged with assaulting a policeman.

Recently Wilson Holmes, Jr., a young Black man in West Philadelphia, seeking extra work to support his family, answered this advertisement in a local newspaper:

More MEN Needed
● Unusual Opportunity ●
● Large Part-Time Income ●
● Gigantic Full-Time Income ●
You may earn as much as
$4–$6 per Hour
with the
Most Revolutionary
New Equipment
No Selling, No Soliciting, No Experience Needed

Applicants should be presently employed, over 21, have a car and not afraid to work. Small investment . . . all of which can be repaid out of earnings. NO CASH NEEDED. ACT NOW.

The man applied for the job, and was put into three days of training, learning to use a floor buffing machine. At the end of the training he was told he "qualified," and that after he purchased a buffing machine the company would refer jobs to him, which would easily pay for the machine. He was taken to a finance company where he "signed some papers," including a judgment note for $1,296. He and his wife were told to stand by the telephone waiting for calls for employment. A week went by and none came. Holmes went back to the company, only to discover the offices vacant and an "out of business" sign on the door. Desperate, he went to the finance company where he begged them to take back the expensive buffing machine and cancel his debt. The company refused, insisting, he said, "You bought the machine—and you have to pay for it." Thus, a man already so burdened by family responsibilities that he in all good faith sought extra income, was legally bound to pay $1,296 for a buffing machine which he discovered was sold elsewhere in the city for $288.75.

When he could not meet payments, the machinery of the law moved in. The Holmeses received this notice, and a similar one was tacked up on the outside of their house: "And ye shall receive a sheriff sale: SHERIFF SALE: Friday July 29, 1966, at 10:30 o'clock A.M., E.D.S.T., 5841 Osage Avenue. Household Goods and Contents. Seized and taken in execution as the property of Elizabeth and Wilson Holmes, Jr., and be sold by William M. Lennox, sheriff."

Ordinarily, the wheels of justice would have moved swiftly and smoothly to rob this man of his property. In this instance, CEPA, as it sometimes can, was able to halt the sale. CEPA rounded up thirty sympathetic neighbors to march in protest in front of the finance company's office. The buffing machine bearing the sign "Worth $288.00, Charged $1,296, SWINDLE" was placed near the curb outside the office. The pickets handed out leaflets to passersby explaining the scheme. It had been merely a racket to sell buffing machines by offering phony employment.

The finance company finally admitted to a delegation from CEPA that Holmes had been swindled. But they disclaimed any responsibility for or knowledge of the swindle. (Under the law, a financial institution is regarded as an innocent "holder in due course" — merely a disinterested party which lends the money, and therefore, except in rare cases, is not responsible to the borrower should the transaction turn out to be shady.) Desiring to end the bad publicity, however, the finance company instructed the sheriff to stop the sale of the Holmes's house, but they refused to cancel his $1,296 debt for the buffing machine. Now Holmes must make regular monthly payments, draining an income he only sought to supplement.

CEPA has been criticized by certain finance companies for bringing pressure through picketing to achieve their ends, instead of going through "proper legal channels." Two automobile companies have been able to obtain court injunctions to stop picketing of their car lots. However, a Philadelphia judge in lifting one of the injunctions said he could see nothing wrong in using "economic pressure" outside the courts. It is almost a necessity, he indicated, for otherwise the consumer is powerless.

Decidedly, in numerous cases, CEPA's picketing has shamed merchants and finance companies into stopping sheriff's sales. However —and this is a sad commentary on the state of our protective laws— when such extraneous pressure has been unsuccessful or nonexistent, countless persons in Philadelphia have lost their homes after being deceived into enormous debt. One man had his house sold by a bank after he missed only one payment. An elderly couple lost their home in a sheriff's sale after they had been tricked into signing a lien on their house as security for a used automobile purchased by their son. He was charged $3,000 for a three-year-old Chevrolet. Others have been driven onto the street, their homes legally stolen and sold at auction because they were duped into subscribing to a food-freezer plan or buying home fire-alarm systems on a phony referral basis. A CEPA official estimates that in Philadelphia County alone, between 200 and 250 homes are put up for sheriff's sale every month. At least half of the for-sale homes, he says, are to satisfy consumer debts, many of them incurred through swindles.

For anyone who would like a brutal testimonial to the daily realities of the marketplace problems of the poor, I would recommend CEPA's monthly tabloid newspaper, *Consumer Voice*. There is a certain impact and unforgettableness in seeing photographs of the victims and their children carrying signs, "Losing Our Home

Due to Misrepresentations," and viewing reproductions of the actual contracts and dunning letters received by the poor. One illustration that stands out as shocking is a collection letter from one of the largest banks in Philadelphia. It was dropped through the mail slot of a couple who had fallen behind in payments of a loan for $225. The man and wife had reduced the debt to $40 when they received the following notice, scrawled in scratchy black capital letters on one of the bank's envelopes:

> WE GUESS YOU WANT
> THE PIG TREATMENT
> AND WE KNOW HOW TO
> TREAT PIGS!
> WE WILL TELL EVERYONE
> THAT YOU ARE NOT
> WORTHY OF TRUST!!

The indignities, terror, violence, despair, and helplessness the poor suffer from deception in the marketplace should weigh heavily on the conscience of America. For the cases reported here are not uncommon; such ill-treatment of the poor by unscrupulous merchants follows a similar pattern throughout the country: in Atlanta, in Chicago, in Denver, in Oklahoma City, in Seattle, in San Francisco, and even in rural areas.

Running throughout this cacophony of deception is a recurring, disturbing theme: the complicity of the law, either seeming or real, in supporting fraudulent business practices, while oppressing the poor and the innocent. Such inhumane treatment from the law appears evident from any economic vantage point, but must be strikingly apparent from the viewpoint of the uneducated, unsophisticated poor, who are left in a whirlpool of confusion by credit practices.

Many of the poor don't understand the most elementary facts of economic life: for example, the role of the finance company. They don't realize that their contract has been sold to an impersonal third party, against which they have no legal recourse. In their simplistic thinking, when the product goes bad or they discover they have been cheated, they refuse to continue payments, thinking this will achieve results. Instead, such action only brings forth the wrath of that strange institution known as the finance company, with its full backing of the law. Refusal to pay often results in a summons to appear in court to offer defense. Some poor, especially the foreign-born, don't even comprehend the summons because of their inability to decipher the legal language. Others never receive the summons at all because of a corrupt practice known as "sewer service." The summons officer, instead of delivering the summons to a ghetto resident, simply throws it in the sewer, leaves it at an old address, or otherwise disposes of it, with the debtor none the wiser. The debtor's absence in court is automatically recorded as default—a confession of guilt. He has forfeited his right to defend himself, and the legal machinery cranks up to enforce payment. Professor Caplovitz found that 97 percent of the court summonses in New York result in default judgment, because of nonappearance.

Unaware of what has happened in court, the debtor is surprised and shocked when the law moves in. A wage earner may get a check with a portion garnisheed; he may be summarily fired, without knowing why; an officer of the law may appear one evening at the door and begin carrying out his furniture. Quite often the law and the merchants or finance companies present an ugly, though perfectly legal, picture of collusion. Routinely in Philadelphia, for example, a deputy sheriff is accompanied by a representative from the finance company when conducting a "sheriff's sale" on household goods. It is not difficult to imagine how the arrival of this twosome in a police car must look to Negro ghetto-dwellers already suspicious of the white man and his law.

Entrapped by devious clauses in contracts and duped by the lies of fast-talking salesmen, many of the victimized poor do not have the faintest notion of what has happened to them; they know only that they have been badgered by bill collectors, lost their jobs, seen their furniture or homes swept away, and that the law is somehow implicated. Worst of all, these poor people are nearly helpless to fight back, for they do not know their rights nor how to exercise them.

One of the worst cases of victimization through ignorance is that of a 56-year-old woman several years ago in Los Angeles, who stood silent and helpless while a local radio shop owner methodically took over her property. Mrs. Elsie Phillips had taken a radio to be repaired, believing it would cost $1, but when she learned the bill was to be $8.90, she dispatched her 20-year-old son to retrieve the radio. Instead, he bought a new radio at payments of $1.25 per week, and Mrs. Phillips signed the sales contract. When payments were not prompt, the dealer obtained a court judgment, ordering return of the radio and $81.50 in court costs and collection fees. It was easy to return the radio, but Mrs. Phillips could not produce $81.50. To satisfy this debt, the dealer then forced sale of her house and lot at public auction. As the only bidder, the radio dealer himself bought the property for $26.50. Mrs. Phillips was allowed to stay on, at $10 a week rent.

A year was required before the deed to the house could be officially turned over to the radio shop owner, and during those twelve months, Mrs. Phillips could have saved her home by paying the $26.50 plus a $25 marshall's fee. But no one had told her, and by the time she found out, the deed had been transferred and there was nothing to do. She simply "sat on the porch of her dingy . . . home," reported *Time* magazine, "and wept."

Faced with similar threats against themselves or their property, most middle-class persons would respond with: "I'll get a lawyer." Persons in poverty, especially minority groups, are so ignorant or leery of the law that they won't seek out legal aid, and sometimes won't even wholeheartedly cooperate when legal redress is offered to them. Neighborhood Legal Services, a nationwide network of offices, funded by the Office of Economic Opportunity, which handles cases for the indigent, reports that their lawyers have great difficulty persuading their clients, mainly members of minority groups, to go to court even when their case is strong. The poor cannot conceive of getting justice from a law which has so viciously exploited them in the past.

In an eloquent statement before the National Conference on Law and Poverty held in Washington, D. C., in June 1965, Nicholas de B. Katzenbach, then attorney general of the United States, summarized the feelings of the poor toward the law: "Too often the poor man sees the law only as something which garnishees his salary; which repossesses his refrigerator; which evicts him from his house; which cancels his welfare; which binds him to usury; or which deprives him of his liberty because he cannot afford bail. The adversary system on which our courts are based fails whenever one side goes unrepresented, and judgment is entered by default.

"Small wonder then that the poor man does not always respect law. He has little reason to believe it is his guardian; he has every reason to believe it is an instrument of the Other Society, of the well-off, of the well educated, the well dressed and the well connected. The poor man is cut off from this society and from the protection of its laws. We make him a functional outlaw. . . .

"Seldom in his struggles with a finance company, a merchant, a landlord, or a rigid official, is the poor man even aware that he has rights which perhaps are being violated. If he knows, he may have no way to protect them. And finally, even if he is aware of legal services, he might well be deterred by irrational fear of cost, shame, or further exploitation."

Despite fears, many of the poor do receive legal aid through Neighborhood Legal Services or other legal aid channels. Sometimes a lawsuit or other court procedure is necessary to obtain justice. But quite often, when confronted by an attorney, the seller who pawned off shoddy merchandise or drew the victim into a deceitful sale will remedy the wrong with suspicious alacrity.

Michael Frank, a former attorney for Washington, D. C.'s Neighborhood Legal Services, explains: "When I say to such a company's attorney, 'It's illegal,' he gives in immediately. Many companies know they are violating the law, but they do it deliberately because they are sure that few poor people will show up in court to defend themselves, and the company will get a default judgment. If they lose a case, the company won't appeal, because they don't want a precedent against them to be set and to appear on the books. It is little matter to these dishonest firms if they lose one small sale or suit. They are still in business, and they have their healthy margin of profit. We catch them on one; they fleece twenty."

The lawyers in Neighborhood Legal Services and other lawyers working in poverty areas are our brightest hope for bringing justice to the poor and deserve unqualified praise for their successes in protecting the indigent from exploitation. Even so, these lawyers themselves recognize that individual victories in court will not cure the cancer or corrupt selling in the ghettos—that legal reform is also essential. Litigation on behalf of a cheated consumer does obtain individual redress. But for every victim rescued, hundreds of others are left to nurse their wrong in silence, or to release their resentment in other ways—perhaps through violence, perhaps through rioting.

Surely there are centuries-old, deeply ingrained social evils, complex and not clearly defined, behind the recent eruption of Negro riots. But one of the evils is generally acknowledged to be the lack of ecenomic equality. We recognize the need to provide blacks with jobs and equal opportunity to help them climb the economic ladder. But we have given too little attention to how these efforts are counteracted when the Negro's buying power is hideously diminished, when he must pay two or three times as much for goods as the rest of society; when the major part of his earnings is dissipated in credit charges; when he is forced by law to fatten the coffers of the men who have cheated and lied to him; when his own property and person are jeopardized by laws that in the measure of their humanity are as outmoded as the debtors' dungeon.

When business and government—in fact, our whole enlightened society—strain to give equal employment opportunities to Blacks, we should also be far-sighted enough to guarantee that his earnings are not stolen from him through unethical business practices and antiquated laws. If we are not, it should hardly surprise us that his resentment might provide one more bit of fuel for the riot fires. Who can forget the television and magazine news coverage of youngsters in Watts, Detroit, Newark (some but ten years old), smashing windows, carrying off television sets and radios, cursing the men who keep their parents in a perpetual state of intimidation, misery, and debt. Memorable are the words of one Watts boy interviewed on television after the rioting. He said:

"Looting and robbing is not the same thing. When you loot a credit store you are just taking back some of the interest they have been charging you for years on them high-priced installment things they sell you on time—$10 down and $2 a week for 900 weeks."

A number of witnesses called before the Governor's Committee investigating the Watts riots did testify that it was not mere coincidence that the prime targets of violence, after the first burst of anger was unleashed, were the establishments of merchants who engaged in sharp selling practices. These witnesses saw a "vengeance pattern" to the destruction of stores in the curfew areas, which they called "a retribution on merchants who were guilty of consumer exploitation. . . .

During the catastrophic Detroit riots in June 1967, arsonists, according to press reports, systematically burned stores known to engage in sharp selling and credit practices. Thirty-two furniture, appliance, and hardware stores, and twenty-three clothing and jewerly stores were destroyed. Reported a columnist for the *Detroit News:* "A Negro woman on relief set fire to a furniture store because she felt she would never be able to pay the bill she owed there. Due to the interest rate, she was being forced to pay $910.12 to satisfy an original debt of $285."

No one would be so myopic as to claim that exploitation by the outlaws of business is the sole cause of racial disturbances. Nor is an opposition to such ruthless exploitation based solely on the possible part it may play in fomenting riots. Simply justice and humanitarianism would demand an end to these practices, even though the consequences were not so evident, nor so serious as riots.

Nevertheless, it seems undeniable that the scandalous gouging of minority groups by dishonest merchants and salesmen contributes to a potentially explosive situation in every ghetto in America and is one of many discontents leading to riots. This is a fact that has been too little recognized or explored. As Caryl Warner, a Los Angeles attorney who handles cases for the poor victimized by shady selling, said right after the Watts riots: "If that committee [the Governor's Commission to investigate the riots] is interested in finding out some of the real causes of trouble, they can come to this office and read a few of my files. . . . When historians write the story of all this trouble, they're going to wonder how in hell such an incendiary element could have been so complacently accepted and overlooked."

Chapter 3

The Law, Morality, and Business

In August 1967, Sidney Margolius, a distinguished writer on consumer affairs for over thirty years, made this observation before the subcommittee on Consumer Affairs of the House Committee on Banking and Currency: "The damage to consumers themselves [from unscrupulous sellers] is greater than many of us may realize. To a large extent—and this may seem a little strong to swallow at first—consumer exploitation has replaced labor exploitation as the real problem of our times."

Former Commissioner Mary Gardiner Jones of the FTC has said: "No matter how informed and sophisticated the consumer, deception will take its toll and the very morality of the community is at stake when there is no effective legal action to be taken against such dishonest merchants."

The President's Crime Commission in its 1967 report warned: "Most people pay little heed to crimes of this sort [consumer fraud

59

and deception] when they worry about 'crime in America' because these crimes do not, as a rule, offer an immediate recognizable threat to personal safety. However, it is possible to argue that in one sense these crimes are the most threatening of all . . . because of their corrosive effect on the moral standards by which American business is conducted [and because they] promote cynicism toward society and a disrespect for the law."

These comments illustrate an awakening to the fact that consumer deception is not merely a small hurt suffered by a gullible few and a minor irritant to legitimate business; *it is a significant social problem.* As the Crime Commission pointed out, consumer deception has traditionally been viewed as of little more import than petty thievery. False advertising, a few misrepresentations here and there, a few dollars stolen from the housewife, have been offenses that up until this time society felt it could tolerate, as we tolerate a number of minor social evils, without fearing that our very morality or societal structure is being jeopardized. This is not to say that we have not found such practices objectionable. The Federal Trade Commission and legitimate business, under the leadership of the Better Business Bureaus, have worked for half a century to eliminate false advertising and deceptive practices. We have long recognized that deceptive selling could harm ethical business. But I am not certain that many of us are yet aware of the real hardships such practices inflict on the consumer or their pernicious effect on society as a whole.

Our attitude, though changing, is still very much "caveat emptor." This is borne out by the fact that we have developed few laws on a wide scale to curtail effectively the gypsters' activities or rectify their wrongs. We have vacillated between treating unscrupulous elements of business as harmless delinquents or hardened criminals—neither of which is a realistic approach. Typically, our defense against unethical businessmen has been warnings to the consumer: advice on how to avoid their wily traps, dissect their phony promises, outwit them. Legislators, district attorneys, the community as a whole, were not moved to red-faced outrage by small-scale, seemingly harmless enterprises such as salesmen pilfering a few dollars from housewives and conning rich widows.

While we were enduring without undue discomfort the escapades of a few villains, the complexion of consumer rackets changed. The credit revolution came. With the phenomenal expansion of credit and installment buying, the unscrupulous could now reach deep into the ghettos and the ranks of the uneducated and unsophisticated to extract large sums. A rich new field was to be found in the mass exploitation of great numbers of the lower and middle classes who knew little about the traps of contracts. Sales were easy to obtain through misrepresentations, and because of the exorbitant credit charges, swindlers could make hundreds or thousands of dollars on a single sale. The thieves formed corporations, organized nationwide rings, used all the modern merchandising methods. What they didn't organize, we organized for them. Our courts and our employers became their collection agencies. Our contract laws, with their outmoded provisions developed to fit the economic conditions of another era, became their instruments of extortion. Our prestigious financial institutions became their financiers.

No one can assess the brutalizing effect of such a system. So new is our awareness of the intensity of the problem that we have made little investigation to find out. But we do know that the victimized are telling us in a hundred ways—including picketing and rioting—that the situation has become intolerable. Mrs. Esther Peterson, when she was special assistant to the president for consumer affairs, made a survey of 30,000 representative letters out of nearly half a million she had received. A thousand of the letters—one in thirty—contained language expressing anger and frustration against a system the writers felt was exploiting them. Wrote a man from Dayton, Ohio: "All we need to understand is that we are dealing with organized dishonesty on a huge scale." Said a woman from Los Angeles: "I do not know whether they [an automobile company] plan to come to steal my car, threaten me with bodily harm, or whether I will pay the bill out of sheer fright. I am frightened."

Repeatedly, I have heard of victims who, lacking legal redress, reverted to jungle law. A number of those taken in by referral schemes have admitted that, in desperation and anger, they mailed referral letters to friends and acquaintances (some ironically headed

"Bonds of Friendship") even *after* they discovered the scheme was a hoax and knew their friends would be swindled too. After the story of Mrs. Phillips, the elderly woman in Los Angeles whose home was sold for $26.50 to her creditor, was publicized in a local paper, four men came to the radio dealer's shop and beat him severely with lead pipes and pistols. In other instances, hysterical victims have tried to shoot the salesman who gypped them, or the collection agent who hounded them. All too often, in despair, the victim turns the gun on himself.

We cannot continue to ignore what, even if no one were protesting, we can see and judge as deplorable offenses to morality. Even one case of injustice is cause of concern to each of us. When such injustice is being practiced on a wide scale, as evidenced by the hundreds of documented cases in the ghettos and thousands among the middle classes, the exploitation transcends individual interest and becomes a problem of urgent, common concern. Responsibility to the injured in society can be denied out of ignorance. But once innocence is dispelled, responsibility is incumbent upon every knowing man, and most certainly upon those in government and business who are in positions of trust and efficacy, and by whose inactions these injustices can continue to exist. As I wrote in the introduction to this book, it can no longer be a question of whether we are going to end this terroristic plundering of the consumer by the outlaws of business, but how we can do it.

Toward this aim our laws must be updated to be truly preventive and not only punitive. Surely in instances where willful intent to defraud is evident, criminal laws should be invoked and such criminal prosecutions will serve as a deterrent to some. However, our primary purpose in consumer protection should be to *prevent* the swindlers from initiating and continuing their lucrative deceptions instead of to concentrate almost entirely, as we have done in the past, on trying to put the wrongdoers behind bars. Also, when a consumer is cheated, we should have some means of redressing the wrong, by restoring his money or freeing him of the debt.

The federal government must take responsibility for formulating and enforcing laws that are needed on a national scale. (Essential reforms in credit legislation are extensive and are discussed separately in the following chapter.) But to the states falls the primary task of curtailing consumer deception. The states possess the greatest potential for quickly detecting and halting the unscrupulous. After seventeen months as the president's special assistant for consumer affairs, Mrs. Peterson was convinced: "The letters that pour into us, the requests from agencies, indicate that the place where the real consumer protection is needed, and where the action is needed, is at the state and local level where the people are. One thing has become very clear—consumer representation at the federal level is not enough. The consumer must also receive representation at the state level and also at the local level."

Paul Rand Dixon, former chairman of the FTC, urged the states "to take business away from us." He has said: "By stopping such practices before they grow into problems of interstate proportions, the need for federal action will be minimized, and the people most directly affected will have a telling voice in deciding what constitutes unfairness and deception. The more effective the states can be in nipping illegal schemes in the bud, the more energy the FTC can devote to dealing quickly and effectively with problems of regional and national significance."

Regrettably, the potential of the states, except in rare instances, is not equaled by enthusiasm, money, or needed legislation. As we have seen, the laws of some states are so inadequate that their citizens have virtually no protection at all outside that offered by the Federal Trade Commission. An analogous situation would be if some states had no laws prohibiting murder, rape, and robbery, and local officials had to wait until a culprit crossed a state line so they could call in the FBI to apprehend him. Lawlessness would prevail, just as it does now in consumer deception.

This is not a situation in which the federal government is alerting states to problems of which they are not already aware. Many state officials, particularly attorneys general who stand "handcuffed" for lack of laws while the gyps run wild, are painfully aware of legislative deficiencies—on both state and federal levels—and soundly support the passage of effective laws.

The ease with which states could assume the legal authority to fight wholesale fraud, if state legislators were so inclined, is phenomenal. The Federal Trade Commission, which is capable of stopping nearly every type of scheme imaginable, operates under a statute singular in its simplicity and brevity. The heart of the statute (Section 45, Title 15 of the U. S. Code) is but nineteen words. It reads: "Unfair methods of competition in commerce, and unfair or deceptive acts or practices in commerce are hereby declared unlawful."

The mark of effectiveness that distinguishes this law from many of the state's criminal statutes is that it is a civil statute aimed solely at stopping deceptive activities without the need to prove the wrongdoer guilty of a crime. Such action is not possible in states which must depend solely on their criminal statutes. Under the FTC law a man cannot be sent to prison; the FTC can simply order him to "cease and desist" from his "unfair, false, or misleading" business practices. If he does not do so, he is subject to civil penalties of up to $5,000 per day for each violation.

Proof of *intent* to deceive is not necessary, and this is the core of the law's strength. The FTC law does not demand that anyone divine the state of a man's mind before requiring him to stop making claims that are false on their face. It is sufficient that the claims are false and are likely to mislead prospective purchasers.

In writing the FTC law (it was first passed in 1914 and amended in 1938), Congress was remarkably far-sighted in making it all-inclusive—not only to meet the unfair and deceptive practices of the day but to cope with future problems, those unforeseen schemes that, as Senator Thomas J. Walsh of Montana said when debating the bill, would inevitably arise out of the "ingenuity of the adroit rogue." Rather than enumerate the schemes to be outlawed, Congress wisely made the FTC law flexible enough to outlaw any deceptive practice—past, present, or future. Through the law, the FTC has been able to prohibit all of the five deceptive schemes discussed in Chapter One. Referral selling has been halted by the FTC act, although the scheme was unknown until several years after the law was passed.

Congress, a quarter of a century ago, put into nineteen words the power to forestall and halt schemes undreamed of. Unfortunately, many state legislatures have not been so far-sighted as to adopt this FTC statute. Only Washington, Hawaii, Massachusetts, North Carolina, South Carolina, Maine, and Vermont have enacted "Little FTC" laws. Several other states, however, including Arizona, California, Connecticut, Delaware, Illinois, Iowa, Maryland, Michigan, Minnesota, Missouri, New Jersey, New Mexico, New York, North Dakota, and Texas, have passed general or fairly general deceptive practices statutes which are similar to the FTC law.

Many state legislatures, instead of following the FTC's lead, continue to pass consumer protection laws on a piecemeal "emergency" basis. In Florida a few years ago it was discovered that used television tubes were being palmed off as new; the legislature responded by passing extensive legislation forbidding such deception—down to requiring TV repairmen to note the condition of the tube as "new" or "used" on sales receipts. The law brought TV tubes under control, but left thousands of other products, equally subject to shady selling practices, completely unregulated. Yet in 1967, the Florida legislature defeated a Little FTC law that would have given across-the-board protection.

Louisiana legislators, after a flurry of concern about deceptive selling of fallout shelters, passed a Little FTC law, but the law applies only to fallout shelters. Kentucky's legislature recently passed three separate pieces of legislation, outlawing referral selling, phony "going out of business" sales, and the use of the term "wholesale" to mean "discount" prices. It rejected a comprehensive deceptive practices law.

So inactive are most state legislatures in passing consumer protection laws that any positive action is to be commended, and separate laws, such as those forbidding referral selling, serve quick, strong notice to the offenders and leave nothing to interpretation; it would be a public service if every state followed Kentucky's crusading lead and flatly outlawed referral selling. Nevertheless, piecemeal legislation alone does not give states the power to keep a jump ahead of the multiplicity of swindles.

Said Senator Walter F. Mondale, when he was the attorney general of Minnesota: "I think there is one [thing] that is too little understood by our state legislatures, and one which must be understood if the states are going to have effective regulation in this field. Most states attack unfair trade practices by specifically proscribing the then known unfair practices, instead of giving [the enforcement] agency the generalized power to promulgate rules in the fashion that they are permitted to do at the FTC level.

"I'm personally persuaded from our experience in Minnesota that you cannot have effective trade regulation unless you have this power of rule-making to permit you to move flexibly and swiftly to develop a modern definition of unfair trade practices as new techniques arise. Because . . . the scope of possible unfair trade practices is limitless. The ingenuity of those who wish to skirt around a statute [makes] the statutes often relatively useless. And if you enforce them, the person against whom you are enforcing them simply will develop a new technique and little if anything is accomplished."

No one would pretend that passage of a Little FTC law will end all consumer protection problems. Several states, and laudably so, have adopted legislation providing powers substantially greater than those afforded the FTC. However, a general deceptive practices statute is as essential in building a state consumer protection program as steel girders are in building a skyscraper. It seems inconceivable that the consumer protection officials of any state, and particularly those in such populous, progressive states as Pennsylvania and Ohio, should have to work under the handicap of no general deceptive practices law. The very minimum of legal protection that citizens are entitled to on a state level is that afforded them in interstate transactions.

The bleak apathy found in most states is even more striking when compared with the spectator activity in a few states, which confirms what Judge Louis Brandeis once said: "It is one of the happy incidences of the federal system that a single, courageous state may, if its citizens choose, serve as a laboratory; and try novel social and economic experiments without risk to the rest of the country. . . . If we would be guided by the light of reason we must let our minds be bold."

Not only one, but several courageous states have developed bold new approaches to thwarting consumer deception. Their vigorous and imaginative use of legislation shows that when apathy is replaced with concern, the gyps can be halted.

The most significant and promising achievement of the states is the establishment of consumer protection bureaus, usually under the attorney general. The pioneering was done in New York under Attorney General Louis J. Lefkowitz, who set up a consumer fraud and protection bureau in 1957. Since then, twenty-seven other states have established consumer protection units of varying effectiveness and power: Alaska, Arizona, California, Connecticut, Delaware, Florida, Hawaii, Illinois, Iowa, Kansas, Kentucky, Maine, Maryland, Massachusetts, Michigan, Minnesota, Missouri, New Jersey, New Mexico, North Dakota, Ohio, Pennsylvania, Rhode Island, Texas, Vermont, Washington, and Wisconsin. The bureaus provide a *centralized* agency through which consumers' complaints can be funneled. Illinois and New York handle about 150 complaints every day. In 1970, Washington's consumer fraud officials received 10,000 complaints, as did California's.

Empowering the attorney general or another state official to bring action against deceptive operators is essential in stopping them before they can fleece hundreds and then move on. Prior to the 1961 Consumer Protection Act in Washington, which established a Consumer Protection and Anti-Trust Division under the attorney general, apprehending swindlers was delegated to thirty-nine prosecuting attorneys statewide. This is still the situation in most states. A culprit chased out of one county could set up business in another. A whole ring of swindlers might work in several counties at a time without being detected. To stop a statewide conspiracy, dozens of separate actions under the criminal fraud statutes had to be brought in many counties. Such cases were time-consuming, amazingly costly (according to a local prosecutor, "One criminal action, as it did in our county, can exhaust the entire annual budget of the prosecuting attorney's office"), and were not guaranteed to result uniformly in convictions.

Under Washington's centralized division, with its network of warnings and communications throughout the state, mobilization against gyps is swift and complete. The attorney general can bring a single case, sweeping up all of a scheme's promoters at once. Once, for example, a multi-state ring of aluminum siding gypsters, chartered in California and headquartered in Portland, crossed over into Washington and infiltrated twenty-two counties. Within fifteen days, proceedings against the company were brought in Seattle's King-County Superior Court, resulting in a halt of their activities. Moreover, and this is another benefit of one intensive effort, many fraudulently obtained contracts and mortgages were adjusted or canceled, amounting to a recovery of $100,000 for the victims.

Art Hansen, a former assistant attorney general in Washington, recalls that when he was a prosecuting attorney he spent "five frustrating years attempting to bring criminal action against a phony furnace company that was making some very vicious sales in our county, and I was never able to do so." But only two months after passage of the 1961 Consumer Protection Act, the attorney general "obtained a consent decree against the Holland Furnace Company, and stopped the problem completely not only in our county but throughout the state of Washington."

To be effective, the attorney general must have strong powers. The primary weapon against gyps is the authority to obtain a court injunction, forbidding the hucksters to continue their fraudulent enterprise. But an injunction requires a trial, and between the time that the swindler's activities are documented and the trial is over, he can accumulate a small fortune, especially if the court's docket is crowded. Some states wisely empower the attorney general to ask a judge for a temporary injunction. This forbids the company to continue the alleged shady selling, pending the outcome of the injunction trial—if there is one. In many cases, the company, when confronted with the prospect of an injunction trial with the resulting publicity, agrees to stop deceptive selling, and rather than argue the case in court, signs a consent injunction.

In Washington and New York, the attorneys general do not always have to go to court to bring a quick halt to consumer exploitation. In lieu of an injunction proceeding, they obtain an "assurance of discontinuance" which is similar to the FTC's assurance of voluntary compliance. The violators must promise in writing to stop their malpractices, and if they break their promise, their very violation constitutes *prima facie* evidence for an injunction against them. Violation of an injunction carries stiff fines for contempt of court; consequently, unscrupulous firms are highly unlikely to violate injunctions. According to the March 1967 *Harvard Law Review,* there is not a single case on record of a firm continuing shady operations after a state injunction.

One of the eternal and perplexing problems in consumer protection is how to take the rewards out of lying. A great many firms work right up until the time the legal ax is about to fall, then give up, and abscond with their ill-gotten profits. Their pocketbooks are undamaged; they cannot be fined unless they violate the injunction. In truth, what we are saying is: "We will let you get away with this once, but if you do it again, we will fine you." Once for some crooks may be enough to last a lifetime. Besides, their profits can be used as capital to set up shop in another state. What we need is a deterrent to entering into consumer fraud in the first place; if we can guarantee that the operators' profits from their incursion into thievery will be taken away, that lying is not lucrative, their incentive will be considerably diminished.

Toward this aim, several states can impose fines (in legal terms, "civil penalties") for misdeeds prior to the time the injunction is final. New Jersey can levy a penalty of $2,000 for a first violation and $5,000 for subsequent violations; New Mexico, $500; Washington State, $2,000 per violation; and California can fine $2,500 for each violation. This deterrent is formidable, if strongly used.

Several states can administer the ultimate *coup de grace,* "corporate execution." They can dissolve a corporation engaging in deceptive practices, or as in New Jersey, put it into receivership, sharing the distribution of the assets with consumers the firm has cheated. New York has dissolved approximately one hundred corporations engaged in deceptive selling. Recently, in New York, after the dissolution of a corporation that deceitfully sold transistor radios, victims of the scheme shared $100,000 of the company's assets.

Several states also make vigorous efforts to see that the cheated consumer is compensated. From 1962, when the Illinois bureau was established, until June 1967, it succeeded through the cancellation of debts and the return of money in saving $1,158,089 for the residents of Cook County (Chicago) alone. New York's bureau in 1970 obtained refunds of $1,471,309 for consumers. Since its creation in 1960, the New Jersey Consumer Protection Bureau has saved consumers close to 4 million dollars in refunds and contract adjustments. Many of these refunds are granted through mediation, not litigation, and are small sums of $5 or $10, usually settlements of misunderstanding with local merchants. Individual mediated settlements are vital in maintaining goodwill and offering redress to consumers. But small-scale individual refunds are not a potent weapon in fighting the inveterate gypster with a large-scale operation.

Undoubtedly, the most efficient justice in cases involving sizeable schemes is obtained through what I call the Robin Hood method: a combination penalty-restitution—taking the profits away from the swindlers and returning them to the cheated consumer. To deal with such swindlers, the attorney general should be authorized—and a few are—to ask in conjunction with the injunction, that the culprit's assets be used, and confiscated if necessary, to reimburse the victimized. This two-pronged justice permits society to penalize, instead of reward, the wrongful seller, and to make amends for the suffering of his victims. It has the added benefit of deterring those who believe they can circumvent justice by making a fast killing before the day of reckoning with the court.

Large-scale court-ordered restitution has not been used as much as one hopes it will be in the future, nor as much as its benefits warrant. New York, Vermont, New Jersey, and California, as permitted by their laws, do often ask for an escrow fund to be set aside to reimburse injured consumers, when obtaining a consent injunction or corporate execution. Illinois, with an excellent law, has an impressive record in the wholesale reimbursements of victims.

After a phony home-repair ring swept through Chicago, William G. Clark, then attorney general, sought an injunction, listing thirty-three complainants who had been victimized. He asked that a receiver be appointed by the court to "take into his possession all the goods and chattels, rights and credits, moneys and effects, lands and tenements, books, records, documents, papers, choses in action, bills, notes, and property of every description, derived by means of any practice declared to be illegal and prohibited by the Act to Prevent Consumer Fraud." A total of $17,000 was collected and apportioned among the thirty-three victims.

The scheme was a particularly reprehensible one. The racketeers convinced an elderly man, after an "engineer" had poured water into the cracks of a concrete basement floor, that water and sewage were collecting under the floor, that the house was sitting on a cesspool and could collapse at any time. He signed a contract for $9,000 and gave the men $4,500 cash. He received $7,500 back from the court. A couple owning an apartment house were instructed by the crooked repairmen not to enter the basement for three weeks or they would be asphyxiated by poisonous chemicals used to exterminate termites. When the time limit expired, they found no work had been done. Two chimneys on their building were left so clogged with bricks and mortar that, according to a gas company investigator, carbon monoxide was not able to escape, and the couple could have been fatally poisoned. These people had $2,750 of their money returned. Sums ranging between $200 and $600 were granted to the remaining thirty-one.

This fraudulent corporation was dissolved, and to prevent the individuals from starting another corporation under another name, the three men were individually named in the injunction, preventing them personally from engaging in such fraudulent schemes in the state of Illinois.

An additional benefit of the court-ordered restitution is that it is but a pebble in the water. It radiates countless other private lawsuits from victims, using the court's decision as a precedent. Officials in both Illinois and New York say that one of the hopes in obtaining a large restitution is that it will generate citizens to take action on their own.

Consumer protection bureaus have also, through the imaginative and aggressive use of existing laws, obtained and helped to obtain precedent-setting court decisions in support of consumers. In a novel interpretation of a law, the Supreme Court of Washington in 1965 declared referral selling a lottery, and hence illegal under the state's anti-lottery laws. The case, *Sherwood & Roberts-Yakima, Inc., v. Leach,* supported by an *amicus curiae* brief from the attorney general's office, was brought by a man and his wife, who had been swindled by a home fire-alarm scheme in which they were to get commissions by supplying the names of friends. The court held that the whole scheme was permeated with chance, that "the respondents took a chance on whether they could get something for nothing." They had no control over the sales operation after they gave the names, in fact were instructed *not* to contact the referrals before the salesman had made his presentation. Thus, they took a chance that the referrals might not be interested, that the salesman might not adequately make his presentation, that the referral might have already been referred by someone else, that the salesman might not even contact the referral.

Furthermore, the court illustrated that the buyers unknowingly took a chance on the market's becoming saturated, and that the whole scheme was absurd:

"The Lifetone salesman told respondents they could get something for nothing through the referral selling scheme. Respondents are obligated to pay $1,187.28 for equipment costing $225.32. For ease of demonstration, respondents must earn twelve commissions of $100 each in order to get, as promised, something for nothing. This means that twelve respondents' referrals must purchase as respondent did; they, in turn, to get something for nothing must find twelve more people to purchase and so forth, as follows:

	Number of Purchasers
	1
1st round	12
2nd round	144
3rd round	1,728
4th round	20,736
5th round	248,832

Soon the scheme will run itself out; the market will become saturated."

Already, by the fifth round, half of the people in Seattle would have had to buy the alarms; taking the court's figures, further, by the sixth round, everyone in the state would have owned an alarm system; by the seventh round, 35,831,808, or the entire population of the Far West; by the eighth round, 429,981,696, or everyone in Europe; and by the ninth round, five billion people, more than all the people on earth.

The court refused to "allow itself to be made the instrument of enforcing obligations alleged to arise out of an agreement or transaction which is illegal." It declared all of the contracts, approximately $130,000 worth, obtained by the illegal referral selling scheme to be void and unenforceable.

In a 1966 decision, New York's Supreme Court (*State by Lefkowitz v. ITM, Inc.*) attacked one of our most widespread, normally untouchable evils: unconscionable sales contracts, under which people are duped into paying 100, 200, or even 1,000 percent more than the merchandise is worth because of enormous credit charges. In the ITM case consumers were sold electric broilers, color television sets, and central vacuum cleaners (that reportedly clean the air of bacteria and dust) on a referral basis; they were promised at least $300 for submitting twenty names, and additional commissions for each referral who "enrolled" in the plan. They were told that six to seven persons out of every ten named could be expected to "enroll." Some victims were left with extravagant dreams of making $9,000 to pay off a house mortgage, plus $1,000 profit; "the earnings were unlimited." The story is familiar. Few referral checks came through, and within ten days the company was dunning purchasers for payments, threatening to sue and garnishee their wages, under agreements that some people had signed without realizing they were sales contracts.

Examination of the contracts revealed that some victims were paying $910 for a broiler that usually retailed for $299; others paid $920 for a central vacuum cleaner that usually cost $350; and as high as $1,575 for a color television set ordinarily costing $600. The judge found these prices and the company's sales practices oppressive, unfair, and shocking to the conscience. The contracts were declared unconscionable under the state's executive law and the

Uniform Commercial Code which states: "If the court as a matter of law finds the contract or any clause of the contract to have been unconscionable at the time it was made the court may refuse to enforce the contract. . . ." The scheme was also defined as a lottery; and the contracts were deemed "utterly void."

The consumer protection bureaus also do a large amount of consumer education—preparing materials for distribution, dispatching speakers, issuing warnings against current frauds. Not only are the bureaus punitive toward unscrupulous businesses, they attempt to be preventive by establishing in cooperation with business, voluntary codes, similar to the FTC's industry guides. New York's code of ethics for the hearing-aid industry has been eminently successful, according to the bureau's director, Barnett Levy. After the code was adopted in 1965, the hearing-aid complaints dropped markedly, although only 40 percent of the state's hearing-aid dealers subscribe to the code.

Not an insignificant function of the consumer fraud bureau is that it becomes a repository of leadership for consumer causes—a powerful lobby in state legislatures. Where consumers were totally unorganized before and their voices rarely heard in the legislative chambers, the consumer bureaus have the knowledge and prestige to convince legislators of the need for innovative legislation to protect consumers. Impressive retail installment acts have been passed in several states, including Illinois, Washington, and Massachusetts, at the instigation of consumer protection bureaus. Some state bureaus have pushed for the licensing of finance companies, correspondence and vocational schools, home-improvement contractors, and television repairmen in efforts to weed out the gypsters by bringing the industry under some state regulation. States without bureaus have also succeeded in passing imaginative consumer legislation. Oregon lawmakers, for example, passed a law to curb telephone solicitations. It requires that the salesman-caller identify himself in the first fifteen seconds, before he can go into his "contest" or free-prize spiel.

It appears certain that states lagging behind in consumer protection not only fall deeper into the shadow of unfavorable comparison, but actually are caught in a deteriorating situation. For, as the fraudulent operators are driven out of one state, they migrate to another with weaker laws. After an injunction put the phony home-repair gang, referred to earlier, out of business in Chicago, they fled to Missouri. Illinois officials notified Missouri's attorney general, who chased them on to another state. At last report they were still in business.

It is probable that unless other states adopt strong laws, they will become the country's reservoirs for swindlers. Already this appears to be true. Henry Helling, chief of Ohio's Consumer Fraud and Crime Section, estimated that in 1970 Ohio consumers lost 300 million dollars through all types of commercial deception. This is one hundred times more than the estimated loss to consumers in Washington State which has strong consumer protection laws. After Washington passed its Consumer Protection Act in 1961, the loss from consumer deception fell to 3 million dollars yearly, as compared with an annual 11 million dollars before passage of the law. (The cost of operating Washington's Consumer Protection Division was about $360,000 in fiscal 1970.)

In fairness, it must be said that many legislators have never considered consumer protection legislation; they are not aware of a problem. In reply to an inquiry about whether one state was considering legislation, an assistant attorney general said: "To my knowledge, the legislature just hasn't thought about it." When I asked a legislator from a midwestern state, known to have more than its fair share of phony operators, what they were planning to do, he was surprised: "We don't have much of a problem out here; if we do, I've never heard about it."

Some legislatures take no action because of an unrealistic fear that business interests will object. Experience shows that ethical businesses have been solidly behind the establishment of consumer protection bureaus, and even more so after they have seen their beneficial effects. In Washington the preliminary citizen's committee that studied consumer affairs and recommended strong legislation and establishment of the consumer division in the attorney general's office was composed substantially of reputable businessmen.

Federally, some changes also need to be made, most urgently, after fifty-four years, in the agency most specifically designated to protect the consumer against deception, the Federal Trade Commission. Of late, the FTC, previously dubbed the "sleeping lady of Seventh Street," has taken some bold new actions, most notably in cracking down on the advertisements and commercials of some of our largest companies. But its new vitality is not matched by its old legal authority.

Deficiencies in the FTC's power often prevent it from curtailing deception as vigorously as it could. New legislation is needed (which I have introduced and which it is hoped will be law by the time readers have this book) to update the FTC.

The new bill gives the FTC the power to seek preliminary injunctions, which some have felt necessary for several years. The FTC's slow processes have proved no match for the whirlwind gypsters who go in and out of business rapidly. (One home improvement company in the District of Columbia was in and out of business in six months, stealing an estimated $250,000, mostly from poor Blacks.) After investigating, the FTC issues a complaint, but a complaint is only a beginning for the FTC, an allegation of deception, and does not compel the company to abandon its deceptive practices. Before a formal cease and desist order is issued, the company may, if it wishes, ask for hearings before an FTC hearing examiner, an appeal before the five commissioners, and a court review. During the proceedings, the culprit can—and some do—stall for time by exhausting all avenues of appeal, meanwhile milking his lucrative business to its final penny.

In response to a senator's inquiry about the "regulatory lag" during hearings, former Chairman Dixon agreed that "if one keeps the case alive going through review to the Supreme Court . . . the promoter can get himself about a four-year period to reap a lot of money." In the case of Mr. G. with his home-improvement operation in Arkansas, the FTC started investigating in 1962, and it was not until 1967, after lengthy FTC hearings and a Supreme Court decision, that he was forced to agree to stop using in interstate commerce the practices proscribed by the FTC.

With the power to seek a preliminary injunction, the FTC could more quickly cut off a dishonest company's business. After compiling enough evidence to warrant a complaint against a company, the FTC would also be able to ask the courts to compel it to cease using the deceptive practices pending the outcome of formal proceedings. Thus, the alleged unfair act or practice could be immediately stopped instead of dragging on for years.

The bill would also offer a potent weapon to deter dishonest hucksters from intentionally taking advantage of the regulatory time lag, by granting the FTC the power to ask the courts to impose substantial civil penalties for first violations when it is found that companies willfully (with intent to defraud) commit a deceptive practice. This is similar to the power which some states now have.

Additionally, the bill would enable the FTC to "take any action necessary to redress the injury . . . caused to the consumer" by those who engaged in deceptive practices. This might include restitution, cancellation of contracts, and so on. No longer would the FTC have to rely merely on a slap of the violator's wrist to maintain fair play in the marketplace. Increasingly, the FTC can be, in addition to its investigative duties, a preventive force.

A recent change in the postal law bears attention because consumers may not have been informed that they are no longer liable for any merchandise sent them unsolicited through the mail. Previously, unsolicited merchandise was one of the nation's largest rackets. A company would send an item—a tie, vitamin pills, stamps for albums, books—through the mail with a bill; then if the receiver did not pay for it, he would be bombarded with dunning letters, the last one threatening a lawsuit. Technically, according to contract law, the recipient was only obligated to pay if he used the item— but many persons paid regardless, believing they had to.

Under the new federal law, which I urged the Senate to pass, such merchandise, if unasked for, is considered a gift, and the recipient has neither to pay for nor return it. He can keep and use it. Any dunning letters or other attempts to collect are a federal crime.

Undeniably, no group is more concerned about consumer protection than ethical business itself. And rightly so. For no one suffers more from widespread dishonesty in the marketplace than the ethical businessman himself. Not only does shady huckstering destroy confidence in the business community generally, but for every consumer cheated, an ethical businessman is cheated. When a consumer is swayed to make a purchase by false promises or deceit from a fly-by-night or unscrupulous salesman, the legitimate dealer loses a sale. Thus, the businessman, like the consumer, is victimized.

It is indisputable that the operation of fraudulent merchants puts ethical merchants at a disadvantage, often a tempting disadvantage. Seeing competitors take away business and pile up profits through a few misrepresentations is enough to strain the morality of many businessmen. It is not easy to remain virtuous when others around you are robbing you of rightful business, making money at your expense—and getting away with it. The most common excuse for using misleading advertising and sharp selling practices is "Everyone's doing it." The New York appliance store salesman who wrote his "confessions" for *Home Furnishings Daily,* as reported in Chapter One, excused himself by saying his tactics were "forced on him by cut-throat competition." The magazine salesman who came to my office complained: "It used to be a more honest business, but now the competition for mass circulation among the top magazines is so great that if you stay honest, you just won't stay in business long."

The responsibility of the business community in fighting gyps is an overwhelming one. And it is a responsibility that ethical business has assumed in the past, and is increasingly assuming. Nevertheless, the potential of legitimate business for reducing consumer deception has certainly not been exhausted. It is especially critical that business follow not only its long-time policy of policing its own members, but that responsible businessmen adopt a policy of *noncooperation* with the unscrupulous.

It is undeniable, for example, that few swindlers could operate without the cooperation of financial institutions. A few of the fraudulent hucksters do set up their own finance companies, or deliberately choose known disreputable financial institutions that will buy their notes and contracts with no questions asked. But it is disturbing, even shocking, to learn that some of our most prestigious moneylending

institutions are supplying the monetary lifelines to fly-by-night outfits and disreputable companies. Some of the contracts in a central
vacuum cleaning referral scheme, which cheated 435 people in the
New York area out of about $400,000 were held by the Chase Man-
hattan Bank of New York City. The First Pennsylvania Banking and
Trust Co. in Philadelphia reportedly bought at least $70,000 worth
of contracts on a referral scheme that swept the ghettos selling fire-
alarm systems. In Yakima, Washington, after the fire-alarm scheme
was declared illegal under the lottery laws, the largest finance company in the city, Sherwood & Roberts, was left holding much of the
paper. It lost about $80,000 when the contracts were declared un-
enforceable.

When an "urban renewal" scheme of home improvements, consisting of an aluminum siding front, swept through Washington,
D.C. several years ago, more than 100 of the contracts were bought
by the Citizens Building and Loan Association of Silver Spring,
Maryland, amounting to about $400,000 worth of FHA-insured busi-
ness. The three perpetrators of the scheme pleaded guilty to fraud,
and in 1971 were given suspended sentences and put on probation.
Nevertheless, Citizens, a small but established firm, continued to collect the fraudulent debts. Many Washington residents were still paying in 1971.

It is true that in few instances do financial institutions have a legal
obligation to check the background and reputation of the sales companies with which they do business. Under "the holder in due
course" doctrine, the bank or finance company can collect and, except in rare instances, is immune from legal responsibility to the
purchaser. Some finance companies state this in a letter to their
customers:

"The Consumer Finance Companies, Inc., cannot accept any responsibility for your purchase; and offers no guarantee that the
representations made to you by the seller of the purchased item is
correct. WE ARE A FINANCING INSTITUTION ONLY. Our only commodity
is money."

Even though financial institutions are legally unaccountable if
they purchase contracts obtained through deception, it seems to me

they have a moral responsibility—a responsibility to the consumer, the community, and other ethical businessmen—to investigate their clients. A reputable bank or a finance company has much better resources than the consumer for investigating the business methods and reputation of a company before buying up hundreds of contracts which may have been obtained through deception. It also has the sophistication to exercise scrutiny and caution. In handing down the decision in New York canceling the unconscionable contracts, the judge observed that the bank that bought them should have become suspicious when it saw that a broiler was being sold for $900 and a television set for $1,500.

All lenders approved by the Federal Housing Administration to grant home-improvement loans have a list of disreputable firms— firms which have failed to perform satisfactorily FHA-insured home-improvement jobs—called a "Precautionary Measure List." The list, which is kept up-to-date (names are continually added, and deleted if the contractor reforms), has at present more than 7,000 names of companies for which the FHA refuses to insure loans, on the theory that it has a responsibility to the public not to be a party to deceit. Thus, every lender handing out FHA-insured home-improvement loans knows which home-improvement companies have acted in an unreliable manner and has a guideline for its judgments in this area.

What are we to think, then, when some lending institutions continue to buy paper from unscrupulous firms on the list? Not long ago, a home-improvement company selling home fronts in the District of Columbia was put on the FHA "Precautionary Measures List" for unconscionable practices, including shoddy workmanship, exorbitant prices, and trickery in obtaining deeds of trust on homes. It is known that at least one bank, unable to grant FHA-insured loans for this company, nevertheless continued to buy its contracts and notes, signed by people who did not have the protection of FHA.

Innocence under "holder in due course," it appears to me, is shattered when lenders knowingly expose consumers to firms which are known by the government to be unscrupulous. All consumers, when possible, should at least be afforded the protection of the FHA's intelligence. When a firm shows up on the "Precautionary

Measures List," the lending institution should at least make a thorough investigation of the company's practices before continuing to do business with it. There will always be those disreputable finance companies that will collaborate with the gypsters; but the reputations of our banks are too valuable and their responsibility too grave to be involved in shady dealings and consumer exploitation—legal or not.

Chapter 4

Closing the Debtors' Prisons

A century and a half ago—during the late 1820s and early 1830s—prisons up and down the Atlantic Coast were filled with tens of thousands of persons, jailed for failing to pay their debts. Shocking as it seems today, many were jailed for debts of less than one dollar and some for as little as one cent. So ill-treated were these prisoners that many were left to rot in dungeons without food or clothing. Hundreds died of starvation and illness. With the coming of Jacksonian Democracy in the 1830s, and 1840s, the debtors' prisons were abolished. Men can no longer be incarcerated for inability to pay debts, and we look with horror on such a cruel system of debt collection. We pride ourselves on having developed humane, socially acceptable methods of enforcing debt payment. Yet, what is humane and enlightened in one era may appear inhumane in the next. Although we have closed the debtors' prisons, in some ways today's consumers are imprisoned by legal methods of debt collection that in our modern context of social values are as destructive and vicious as the debtors' dungeons.

Americans now work millions of man-hours to pay for outrageously priced merchandise and enormous credit debts that they were deceived into buying, and in some cases do not even possess, as in the case with the repossessed stoves in Cleveland. Mr. Gallman in Philadelphia, whose furniture was confiscated, labored 1,120 hours at $1.25 per hour—or a total of twenty-eight weeks—to pay for an overcharge of $1,400, including $1,000 finance charges forced on him by trickery. Such a travesty—in effect working in slavery without receiving any benefit from his earnings—would never be allowed under our labor laws. As writer Sidney Margolius noted: "We would not permit the things to be done to people as workers that we allow to be done to them as consumers."

One of the purposes of abolishing the debtors' prisons was to allow men to work to earn money to pay off their debts. Yet, thousands of people have been fired because employers did not want to bear the bookkeeping costs of processing wage attachments. It appears that under our modern system we have in many cases substituted joblessness for imprisonment.

Countless persons have lost their homes and all of their possessions for minor debts. We would be outraged about imprisoning a man for a petty debt. Still, we allow his home and furniture to be sold to satisfy debts of as little as $25. We would not let a man be imprisoned without a trial. Yet consumers are deprived of millions of dollars worth of their property at the whim of the creditor without any judicial proceedings whatever.

Clearly, our system of debt enforcement, especially our contract laws, was never meant to deal with the kind of widespread consumer credit that has burgeoned in the last quarter of a century. As Barbara Curran points out in her comprehensive study *Trends in Consumer Credit Legislation,* laws governing credit grew "like topsy," in fragmented, snail's pace fashion. "It is not surprising," she writes, "that developments in the law have failed to keep pace with the mushroom-like growth and expansion of consumer credit itself. Nor is it surprising to find that efforts aimed at dealing with specific problems which have arisen at various stages and in particular phases of development of consumer credit have been ad hoc in nature."

Nor is it surprising that changing times have left our credit laws skewed far toward the benefit of the seller. Mostly responsible for the modern-day imbalance in the legal rights of the buyer and seller is the historical basis of contract law. Our whole legal doctrine which governs contracts is based on a presumption that both parties are of equal ability to realize the consequences of the transaction and fulfill them. At a time when the credit-buying system was highly sophisticated and those trading with each other were usually businessmen and usually on an equal footing with each other, it was reasonable to expect credit buyers to exercise match-wits caution. Rare was the man forty years ago who completed a big transaction without days to study the papers, usually with the help of an attorney. Today, millions sign installment contracts of tremendous legal consequences, often without reading or understanding them, after only ten minutes thought. It is ludicrous to suppose that a buyer with no knowledge of the law is on a par with a dealer whose sophisticated lawyers have meticulously worded the contract to the undisputed advantage of the seller. Yet the law continues to operate as if the credit revolution wrought no changes at all in the buyer-seller relationship, as if that one-time equality still exists.

Our credit laws have become obsolete to deal with the current situation, and it is apparent that we need a comprehensive reappraisal of our whole system of debt collection, including contracts, with a view toward reestablishing a balance in the bargaining power between buyer and seller. No one would want to establish a system in which a man could avoid his rightful debts. Society must retain reasonable and enforceable threats against the man who would falsely incur debts, and willfully or irresponsibly refuse to pay them. Surely the soundness of our vast credit-buying system demands assurances that consumers can be forced to pay, for no society can long tolerate economic lawlessness. But the soundness of any system does not demand, nor can it long tolerate, the enforcement of injustices against its citizens. Allowing such a system to persist can only lead to a crumbling of confidence in society and the law.

To assure justice, many of our contract clauses and debt-collection practices that allow consumer exploitation must be abolished or reformed. The problem of such reform is indeed complex. One cannot risk weakening creditor remedies to the point of ineffectiveness. Yet, we are not absolutely certain how important creditor remedies are in the total credit picture. Deprived of easy credit collection, would some sellers clamp down on the extension of credit to the detriment of the economy and to the detriment of some consumers who seemingly need credit to maintain a decent existence? There is no evidence that this would happen, although certain sellers, wanting to maintain the status quo, speculate that it would.

It seems to me that it would more likely create a renewed responsibility in the extension of credit which would be beneficial rather than harmful. Although the wise use of credit makes possible a higher standard of living for most of us that would otherwise not be immediately attainable, the misuse of credit plunges many into helpless and needless debts and creates an atmosphere of irresponsibility.

Today's credit debt stands at an astounding 127 billion dollars, excluding mortgage credit. The interest and finance charges on this consumer credit debt is 17 billion dollars, almost as much as the interest payments on the entire 416 billion dollar federal debt. Americans have a remarkable record of repaying debts. Less than 1 percent of all debts finally are marked off as uncollectable. Nevertheless, a few contract to buy with no intention of repaying. And many merchants sell *knowing* full well the customer cannot repay. The goods are repossessed, wages are garnisheed, bankruptcy is filed. Clive W. Bare, a bankruptcy referee in the eastern district of Tennessee, appraised the situation precisely when he said recently: "Clearly too much credit is being extended today, and too many loans are being made not on the basis of a debtor's character, integrity, or ability to pay, but solely because the lender or creditor knows if the debtors do not pay, their wages can be attached."

This is irresponsibility of the most pernicious kind, and if reforming debt-collection measures would have the effect of making creditors scrutinize their debtors more closely, it would be desirable. It is also probable that a clampdown on the easy collection methods that make fraudulent schemes possible would rechannel wages back into legitimate sources, benefiting the ethical businessman and harming only the unscrupulous fast-dealer.

There are some who fear that reforming debt collection would inflict suffering on the poor who would no longer be able to obtain credit for necessities. If this proved to be a problem, it would be far more humane and wiser to develop credit outlets for the poor, such as neighborhood credit unions where interest is low, than to continue to saddle the poor with offensive collection practices which cheat and oppress them by subjecting them to abusive interest and finance charges of 100 percent or more.

Another question without an answer is: What effect will abolishing or revising some debt-collection methods have on the use of others? For debt collection has not one but an arsenal of weapons—garnishment, foreclosure, repossession—which are interdependent in an unknown relationship. It is my guess that creditors will always find an ingenious method of collection, and we must be careful that by abolishing one, we do not give rise to other alternatives, even more destructive. A comprehensive, long-term, scholarly study on the interrelationship of credit remedies would be worthwhile. In the meantime, we can only proceed on existing knowledge with a sense of justice as a guide. It seems to me that reforms must be made in a number of areas before we can say that the debtors' prisons of the mid-twentieth century have truly been closed.

Garnishment

The personal hardships and economic destruction caused by this coercive instrument of debt collection cannot be overestimated, despite recent reforms in garnishment through the federal Truth in Lending Act. In July 1970, a federal law went into effect to modernize garnishment nationwide by setting a limit on how much could be garnisheed from a paycheck and prohibiting a person's being fired as a result of a single garnishment.

Previously, garnishment was regulated entirely by the states, and the amount that could be garnisheed varied widely. In some states the amount that could be taken from wages was so oppressive that a worker had little or no money left to live on. For example, a man and his wife in Cleveland, Ohio, were left with $10 a week with which to buy food after his night watchman's salary of $89.56 per week was garnisheed. Oregon, Tennessee, Utah, and Minnesota allowed 50 percent of a worker's wages to be confiscated for garnishment. Other states had minimum cash figures which were "untouchable." Vermont guaranteed garnisheed persons only $30 per week plus 50 percent in excess of $60 per week. Virginia allowed a maximum exemption of $35 per week for heads of families.

Washington State had one of the harshest laws. A single person with no dependents was allowed to keep only $25 a week maximum, which on a weekly salary of $100 would be 25 percent. Those with dependents were allowed an exemption of $35 per week, plus $5 for each dependent, but the maximum granted was $50 per week. Thus a man with six children could take home but $200 monthly if garnisheed.

Several persons finding themselves unable to support families on the pittance left after garnishment committed suicide. Many others continued to pay off unjust debts through garnishment for fear of losing their jobs. In dramatic testimony, before passage of the bill, Willard Wirtz, then Secretary of Labor, estimated that as many as 300,000 workers a year were fired because their employers did not want to bear the cost of processing garnishments. Other authorities, including Judge George Brunn of Berkeley, California, presented figures showing that garnishment was directly related to the alarming increase in personal bankruptcies. Judge Brunn also found that there was a distinct correlation between the harshness of the state's garnishment provisions and the number of bankruptcies.

In a classic study, "Wage Garnishment in California: A Study and Recommendations," for the *California Law Review* in December 1965, documented this relationship. He compared the garnishment laws of the ten states with the highest bankruptcy rates for 1962 with the ten states having the lowest bankruptcy rates. He found that Texas had only two bankruptcies per 100,000 population; Pennsylvania, four; Florida, North Carolina, South Carolina, and South Dakota, which authorize exemptions up to 100 percent if needed to support the debtor's family, had respectively seven, one, three, and eleven bankruptcies per 100,000 population. New Jersey allowed

90 percent exemption and had a bankruptcy rate of twelve per 100,000 population; Alaska granted a $350 exemption for married debtors and had a rate of thirteen. In comparison, Alabama, with only a 75 percent exemption, had 279 bankruptcies per 100,000 population; Oregon, with a $175 exemption, had a rate of 200; Arizona, with a 50 percent exemption, had a bankruptcy rate of 147; California, also with a 50 percent exemption, had a rate of 145.

Moreover, proving that such relationship was not due to chance, Brunn pointed to the experiences of Illinois and Iowa. In 1961, when Illinois liberalized its exemptions, its bankruptcy rate dropped. In three years, it declined 9 percent, while the national average rose 18 percent. Conversely, when Iowa in 1957 abolished its 100 percent exemption in favor of an inadequate $35 per week, plus $3 per dependent, bankruptcies soared at an astonishing rate, quadrupling between 1957 and 1963.

It was thus indisputable that debtors were being driven into bankruptcy under pressure from harsh garnishment laws.

With these facts in hand the drive for garnishment reform grew, climaxing in the federal provisions of 1970. It was decreed by Congress that 75 percent of a worker's wages or thirty times the minimum hourly wage, whichever was higher, was safe from garnishment. Although at this writing the law has been in effect only one year, it is apparent that the scourge of garnishment has not been removed; in fact, one might say, it has hardly been touched. Garnishment is still economically oppressive—the loss of 25 percent of one's income, particularly to those living marginally, can be a catastrophe; encourages the payment of unjust debts; and fosters personal hardships.

Although the exemption of 75 percent from a creditor's hands may seem liberal, actually it is not, and many consumer groups urged at the time of the law's passage that the exemption be 90 percent. In some respects garnishment was more liberal when it was introduced one hundred years ago. In the nineteenth century, to quote a bankruptcy referee in the federal district court in Louisville, the garnishment law was "probably the most progressive law in the country." It was seen as a humane alternative to the debtors' prisons, as well as a boon to the creditor, who could now collect his debts instead of watching the debtor rot away in the debtors' prisons without earning a cent. Exemptions were often higher then than the exemption called for today by federal law.

For example, in 1910, an enlightened Kentucky legislature allowed garnisheed workers to keep $67.50 per month when the prevailing wage was $75, which is 90 percent. Additionally, the thirty times the minimum wage of $1.60, provided by the federal reforms, works out to $48 a week, lower than some welfare checks.

It is instructive also that many states at the time of the law's passage already had far more lenient garnishment laws. These states are allowed to apply for exemption from the federal statute so as not to downgrade their provisions. A compilation by the Department of Labor, made right after the law was passed showed that twenty-three states had exemptions higher than those required by the new law. Florida prohibited garnishment on any wages on the head of a family. Hawaii exempted 95 percent of the first $100 a month, 90 percent of the next $100, and 80 percent of the balance. New York and New Jersey exempted 90 percent, Louisiana and West Virginia 80 percent, while the federal standard is 75 percent. It must be said, however, that the federal law is superior to that of most states in other respects, for example, in the set minimum exemption of $48. Previously, some states had no minimum at all.

With an exemption that was no better than what half of the states already had, one wonders what effect, if any, the federal law will have on curbing personal bankruptcies, one of the strong arguments used in its passage. It would appear that Judge Brunn's figures would stand, although it is too early at this writing for a new study to be made. If people were being driven into bankruptcy faster in states like Alabama that had a 75 percent exemption than in New York with a 90 percent exemption, then it would appear the trend would continue as long as the situation exists.

Additionally, some persons felt that setting a standard exemption by Congress would "institutionalize" the 75 percent as a national norm, causing some states to retrogress and reduce exemptions to the minimum legal requirement. So far only one has gone backward: Nebraska reduced its exemption allowed heads of families from 90 percent to 85 percent. On the whole most states have substantially improved, some continuing through legislative action to rise above the national standard set by law.

Enforcing the law is also difficult—a task given to the Labor Department. In the first year the law was in effect, Labor Department compliance officers found that out of 255 firms investigated in a check of ten cities, 134 of them had instigated or processed illegal garnishments, either taking out too much or levying a garnishment when they shouldn't have. Most of these involved financial institutions. Labor Department officials estimate that these figures encompass about 3 to 4 percent of the businesses under their jurisdiction. Some firms even escape Labor's scrutiny for they do not come under the Fair Labor Standards Act—for example, retail businesses doing less than a quarter of a million dollars worth of business a year. Thus, some violations may escape unnoticed unless an individual complains.

Persons are also still being fired for garnishments despite prohibitions. Labor figures show that during the first year, fifty-three establishments discharged employees for garnishments. Thirty-four fired employees were rehired, following complaints.

Aside from how much is garnisheed from a paycheck, there remains the question: Should we tolerate garnishment at all? Garnishment is frequently and viciously used as a club to force payments of unfair debts. When used by the unscrupulous in such manner it provides police power; in truth a public subsidization for the collection of wrongful debts. "The county sheriff becomes a backstop for the salesman," as one consumer authority phrased it.

So fearful are many wage earners even of the *threat* of garnishment that they would rather pay than complain. Often a phone call from the creditor to the debtor's employer is sufficient to compel payment. In a recent study, Professor David Caplovitz found that 44 percent of the default-debtors said their employers had been contacted and warned about garnishment proceedings; many of the debtors, reported Dr. Caplovitz, resumed paying even though they believed they had been cheated.

The personal hardships of garnishment are often overlooked. In

1965, a home-improvement company came into Washington, D. C., and two sisters, among 700 others, signed up for a "towne house front" for $4300. They insisted the work was shoddy, that it cost $2000 more than they had been told, and that they had not to their knowledge signed a promissory note. Two years later, both of them, working as maids in hotels had their wages garnisheed. In mid-1971 they were still paying, although the three principals had pleaded guilty to fraud. The two women because of their garnishment were cruelly discriminated against. They could get no credit anywhere; their credit rating was ruined, and they were forced to remain at their present jobs, fearful that no one would hire them with the garnishment in effect. Every time they received a paycheck they hated the garnishment anew, and were so in despair of paying it off that they said bitterly, "Our social security checks will probably be garnisheed."

On the basis of present evidence, it appears to me that the best reform may well be abolition of this practice altogether. I am convinced that as the evils of garnishment become more widely recognized, Congress will be forced to consider outlawing it just as they outlawed debtors' prisons a century and a half ago.

An important consideration is: What effect—if any—would abolishing garnishment have on the extension of credit? Some predict that credit would be sharply withdrawn, and it is not difficult to imagine that proposals for abolishing debtors' prisons also brought forth dour predictions that the economy would collapse. That the abolition of garnishment, however, would have any effect on the granting of credit is highly improbable. Evidence indicates that merchants would grant credit as usual and employ other methods of collection, including dunning letters, repossession, liens on property, attachment, and execution levies against cars, bank accounts, and homes. We have only to look to such states as Pennsylvania and Texas, where garnishment has been outlawed for a century, to observe that they are not suffering from a lack of prosperity. Nor are members of the armed forces or federal government employees unable to obtain credit, although they are immune from garnishment. If garnishment were a factor in inhibiting credit, one would expect to find that the ratio of consumer credit to retail sales would be high in states with harsh garnishment laws and low in states with liberal provisions or no garnishment at all. Figures from the Associated Credit Bureaus of California for 1963 revealed that about the *same* amount of credit was extended in states, regardless of the severity or leniency of garnishment laws. California and New York, for example, have comparable populations and total personal income. California had exceptionally harsh garnishment provisions (50 percent exemption), and New York had extraordinarily liberal ones (90 percent exemption). Yet, in 1963, 6.6 billion dollars worth of installment credit was extended in California and 6.1 billion dollars in New York. Installment sales represented 24.6 percent of the total retail sales in California and 25.5 percent in New York.

The percentage of credit given in 1963 in Texas, which outlaws garnishment, was about the same as that in New York, California, Colorado, and Alabama (the last two also had severe garnishment provisions). The ratio of installment credit to retail sales in Alabama was 24.4 percent; in Colorado, 25.1 percent; and in Texas, 25.3 percent.

Nor does the per capita income of a state vary in direct proportion to the state's garnishment laws, as, according to Judge Brunn, could be expected if the absence of this threat did, as claimed, damage the economy. The citizens of California and New York have about the same incomes; so do those of Pennsylvania and Ohio (with a harsh garnishment law) and those of Florida and Vermont (which also had a stringent law).

After analyzing these and other facts, Judge Brunn concluded in his garnishment study that there is no observable link between the availability of credit and the absence or presence, or stringency or leniency, of garnishment.

What about garnishment for taxes, alimony, and child support? I believe we will have to make exceptions here with certain safeguards, for these, as distinguished from commercial debts, are debts to society, on which the functioning of the government and children's lives may depend. Additionally, those whose wages are garnisheed for taxes are often in high income brackets, for example, entertainers, whose income may be in the six figures. Nevertheless, reforms would have to be adopted for those garnishees to prevent job loss and inhumane wage attachments. Certainly the government should not be permitted to confiscate all of a man's paycheck, as happened to the auto-worker from Indiana, nor amounts that may cause severe hardships. Vern Countryman, a professor at Harvard Law School, recommends that at least $15,000 of a person's annual income should be immune from garnishment. It has also been suggested that garnishment exemptions be on a sliding scale to income, as income taxes are.

Garnishment abolition or reform must be accompanied by similar action on wage assignments. This is different from garnishment in that it supposedly occurs "voluntarily." Creditors insert in contracts a clause which states that in case of default the signer will turn over his wages through "voluntary assignment" to the creditor. As in garnishment, the creditor can then legally attach the debtor's paycheck.

A loophole in the recent Truth in Lending legislation is its failure to put any restrictions on wage assignments. Officials suspect, although it is too early to be certain, that many of the same evils once attendant on garnishment are now cropping up increasingly with wage assignments. Some states that will not allow more than 25 percent to be garnisheed permit much more to be confiscated through wage assignments. It would be surprising if creditors did not then turn to wage assignments.

It is certain that persons are also being fired for wage assignments, although figures on the number are difficult to obtain. For wage assignments are just as costly to employers as garnishments. Decidedly, a study needs to be done on the disastrous effects of wage assignments, particularly to determine if some of the garnishment reforms are being negated by an increase in abuses in wage assignments.

We should make no mistake about it: eliminating garnishment and wage assignments is not a cure-all, as is evident from the gouging of consumers in Pennsylvania where garnishment does not exist. In the absence of garnishment, foreclosures on homes are more prevalent; repossession is more vicious. Jeopardizing a man's home instead of his job would be no improvement. Thus, the abolition of garnishment alone could be harmful. It must be accompanied by other credit reforms that will prevent even worse debt-collection methods from filling the vacuum left by garnishment.

Confession of Judgment

Many outrageous consumer abuses would be checked in a court of law were it not for "confession of judgment," which is legal in installment credit agreements in about twenty states. First to outlaw it were California, Connecticut, Maryland, Massachusetts, Minnesota, New Hampshire, New Jersey, New York, and North Dakota. By signing an installment contract or promissory note containing this provision, a purchaser waives virtually all of his rights to due process of law and to a judicial review of whether the debt was just. In effect, he delivers all of his legal rights into the hands of the creditor.

As shown by a typical confession of judgment clause, he agrees to "irrevocably appoint any attorney of any court of record attorney for me . . . to confess judgment in favor of the seller against me." (It is interesting, but perhaps not surprising, that in some cases the attorney who pleads guilty for the debtor is the same attorney who brought suit for the creditor. This conflict of interest is not illegal, although it hardly advances the cause of justice.)

The consumer agrees to "waive issuance of process and service thereof, to waive trial by jury. . . ." Thus, he has no opportunity to meet the creditor in court face to face, or to try to persuade a judge that the debt is unjust. He is not even notified of the judgment against him. Some victims of the appliance store rackets in Cleveland did not find out until they received a paycheck that had been garnisheed. In Philadelphia many people who had signed judgment notes did not know that their house was up for auction until the "sheriff's sale" notice arrived in the mail.

The debtor usually agrees to the added indignity of "reasonable attorney's fees" for his own "representation" in court, as well as that of the creditor. (In Illinois, "reasonable" fees are usually 15 percent of the balance of the debt. A man who owed $3,000 on a car before judgment owed $3,450 afterward, including $450 legal fees.) The attorney does little more than sign his name, sometimes with a rubber stamp.

If there were errors in the original contract or the proceedings, which might be used for his defense, the buyer agrees to "waive and release" those too, "hereby ratifying and confirming all that said attorney may do by virtue thereof." In 1966, Attorney Jerome Schur at the request of Chief Judge John S. Boyle of the Circuit Court of Cook County, did a study of 1,305 cases in the Court's Municipal Division in which creditors obtained judgment under confession of judgment clauses. The study disclosed a number of irregularities in filing the confession of judgment suit: attorneys claimed fees they were not entitled to; some signed with a rubber stamp (showing "the assembly line technique which stresses speed rather than exactness," commented the investigator); some judgment claims were not notarized; some were not even signed, but the blank line was notarized anyway; and in one case a contract was processed that did not even possess a confession of judgment clause.

In four contracts, the number of payments when multiplied by the monthly sum came to more than the total balance. In others it appeared the contract had been tampered with. In thirty-four cases, the contract was completed in more than one color ink; in four cases it was completed in both print and script; in twenty-six cases it was filled out in pencil; twenty-nine judgment notes contained blank spaces, which is contrary to Illinois law. Despite these inaccuracies, possible fraud, and sloppy attention to the fine points of law, if the court does not detect the error before the judgment is entered, it stands. And, as Mr. Schur points out, the court is so overburdened by the number of judgment suits that meticulous examination is no longer possible.

Immediately, after a customer signs the note or contract, the creditor records the judgment in court, accompanied by an affidavit to its authenticity and a small fee, sometimes $5. The creditor thereafter can ask for an execution on the note, demanding full payment according to the provisions. The court grants the judgment *automatically* without consulting the debtor or hearing any defense he may have to offer. If the workmanship is shoddy, if the company fails to complete the work, if the merchandise falls apart, if it was sold through fraud, the debtor pays regardless. By signing, he has agreed to pay the debt regardless of extenuating circumstances. He has prejudged himself guilty.

Interestingly, the confession of judgment, like garnishment, was once a legal device to benefit the poor. Legally, *cognovit* means: "An acknowledgement or confession by a defendant that the plaintiff's cause, or a part of it, is just, wherefore the defendant, *to save expense,* suffers judgment to be entered without trial."

Today, cognovit in the hands of many credit merchants has become a malicious instrument of extortion, enabling creditors to collect unjust debts and to shift the ordinary costs of doing business to the very people they victimize and to society as a whole through our court system. It is understandable why some financial interests support this distortion of justice, for it relieves them of many responsibilities, hazards, and expenses. It obviates the necessity of checking to determine if a man is a good credit risk, for they know, even if their extension of credit is outrageously unsound, he *must* pay without argument. As one finance company in Pennsylvania admitted, "it saves us attorney's fees; there are no complaints to file, no defenses to overcome, and no chance that the court might decide the money is not due." The proceeds of a bad debt need not even be shared with a collection agency. Our courts collect the entire debt promptly, efficiently, and for free.

The cognovit provision is widely used. Before a change in the law, from 300 to 500 confessions of judgment were recorded every day in Philadelphia's City Hall—nearly 150,000 a year. In the two-week period—from June 20 through July 1, 1966—studied in Cook County, $848,338.44 in debts was legally turned over to creditors through confession of judgment. If this period is average, as the investigators believe it is, *an astounding 22 million dollars worth of debts is collected yearly in Cook County by confession of judgment,* and 34,000 persons every year are coerced into paying without being allowed a murmur of protest in court against possible injustices of the debts.

That some victims might have just cause for complaining, had they not signed away their rights, was further documented by Mr. Schur's study. Some creditors did not even give their debtors a reasonable opportunity to pay. In twelve cases the creditors executed the confession of judgment *within two months* after the contract was signed. One hapless debtor was struck with a judgment suit seven days after he had signed a contract, *even before the first payment was due.*

So offensive are the abuses of confession of judgment that its use in consumer installment contracts and notes should be outlawed by the states or, if necessary, by Congress. In our judicial system every man has the right to be served in court, to have a trial, to present evidence, to take depositions, to cross-examine witnesses, before he is judged guilty or not guilty. We do not send a man to jail without giving him the right to a trial. We should not deprive him of his home, his wages, his possessions, without the right to trial. Such a systematic deprivation of rights is morally unjustifiable.

The legitimate merchant with a legitimate claim should not fear to face a debtor in open court. The reputable sellers, however, who investigate their clients, are not the primary users of confession of judgment. In the Cook County study, nearly half of all the suits brought for radios, TV's, and hi-fi's came from one store on West Madison Street.

Outlawing confession of judgment will not, we should recognize, accord everyone judicial review of the fairness of a debt. Its abolition will be a monumental victory in freeing the citizens of many states from a legal bondage to unscrupulous sellers. But, as we have seen in New York, which does not allow confession of judgment, 97 percent of all the suits still result in default judgment because the debtor does not come to court to defend himself. Thus, the right to defend oneself can also be defeated through ignorance, sometimes through illegal shenanigans locally in which the court summons is never served. These problems show the need for increased public awareness which will spur a reform of local court procedures and intensive efforts to encourage people, especially the poor, to take advantage of their legal rights. Neighborhood Legal Services, OEO-funded credit unions for the poor, and many community groups are vital in guaranteeing these rights. Without education of the poor and the unsophisticated, even the best system of legal protection will flounder.

Deceptive Contract Provisions

Other installment credit practices that should be forbidden by law are the acceleration of payments without cause, balloon payments, and add-on purchases. According to some contracts, the creditor can, without giving a reason and in the absence of default payment by the purchaser, arbitrarily accelerate payments, insisting on the total balance immediately. Failure to pay the total sum can result in garnishment of wages, foreclosure on property, repossession of the merchandise, and other hardships.

This contract provision produces some especially ugly consequences when used in conjunction with confession of judgment; it puts a consumer at the complete mercy of a creditor's disposition. A person who buys on the installment plan should be assured that both parties are obligated to carry out the bargain in good faith and that the only demands on the buyer are to pay the regular monthly payments, as he is led to believe.

Such a fairness doctrine should also pertain to balloon contracts. Most credit buyers understandably assume that when they are told they owe $77 per month, that is the amount they pay monthly until the debt is satisfied.

Some contracts, however, provide for a frightening final surprise. When the debtor comes to the end of several years of the small monthly payments, he is confronted with one enormous payment of perhaps hundreds or occasionally even thousands of dollars. The payment has suddenly ballooned, thus the term "balloon contract," and unless he can produce the final lump sum, he is put into a squeeze: he faces either the loss of his possessions, sometimes including his house, or refinancing the debt, which means he is paying interest on interest, usually at exorbitant rates.

Some unscrupulous dealers use balloon contracts to deceive purchasers into signing up for merchandise they cannot afford, under the guise that it is "only a few dollars a month." In the District of Columbia one fifty-six-year-old woman bought four air conditioners, worth about $970, for about $2,000. This scheme also involved duping homeowners into signing mortgages. The woman discovered later that unknown to her, in order to pay the debt, she had mortgaged her house for $5,800, on which she agreed to pay 7 percent interest in sixty monthly installments of $33.50, plus a final balloon payment of $5,000. Thus, in five years the woman could have paid off only $2,010, little more than the interest. At that time the creditor could foreclose on the house or refinance the loan.

Under the same financial arrangements, investigators determined that she would not have been able to pay off the debt in her lifetime. Thus, the creditor could have kept her debt-indentured, grinding out interest, and in the end taken the house. Fortunately, this woman arranged a settlement through court.

How people can be milked dry by balloon contracts was further illustrated by the case of another D. C. woman who had her debts consolidated by a company that advertises itself as "private bankers." She signed a balloon note for $3,000, but actually received only $1,500. Unable to pay, she was forced to refinance it with a finance company, this time signing a note for $5,290 and receiving less than $3,000; she understood she was to pay if off at sixty payments of $77; she was not aware of the final balloon payment of $1,800. As security for the loan, she had signed a deed of trust on her home, which she risked losing if she could not make the final payment. As that dread day drew near, a home-improvement salesman who just "happened to be in the neighborhood and noticed that her home needed repairs," dropped in one Sunday afternoon and, learning of her predicament, offered to make certain home improvements and pay off her other debts if she would sign a contract for $3,980. She did. The nature of this unconscionable racket was revealed when it was discovered that the man from the "bank" who gave her the first loan was a brother of the agent of the finance company who consolidated her second loan. And both of these were brothers of the director of the home-improvement company who coincidentally arrived just in time to "rescue" her by luring her deeper into debt.

Although it is possible that for some persons with seasonal occupations and irregular incomes the balloon contract is a convenience and its use may be justified in special instances, it should otherwise be forbidden. For it is misleading, is not executed in good faith, makes the signer vulnerable to unexpected disaster, and perpetuates the debt treadmill. Its primary goal is clearly victimization.

One of the most outrageous methods of victimization is through the prorated or add-on contract. To be most lucrative, the scheme is worked this way: when the debt for one piece of merchandise is nearly paid off, the seller induces the customer to make another purchase, which is then added on to the original contract; when the balance is low again, he invites yet another purchase, also adding that to the contract, and so on. If the buyer defaults on a payment, after what can be years, the seller can repossess *all* of the merchandise listed on the contract, for instead of applying the payments to cancel out the debt on any one purchase, he has prorated them among all the purchases, leaving a small balance due on each item of merchandise.

In a famous case, *Williams v. Walker-Thomas Furniture Company* of Washington, D. C., Mrs. Ora Lee Williams beginning in 1957 bought several items from the store on installments. She faithfully made payments. In April 1962, when she had reduced her balance to $164, the store sold her a stereo record player for $514.95. Soon after she was unable to make payments, and the company fell back on a clause in her contract that stated: "All payments now and hereafter made by (purchaser) shall be credited pro rata on all outstanding leases, bills, and accounts due the Company by (purchaser) at the time each such payment is made." The company then repossessed everything Mrs. Williams had bought from them since 1957. After $1,400 in payments, she was left with nothing. In a landmark decision, the court declared that the contract could be held unconscionable.

We should go further and declare that add-on contracts are legal only when payments are allocated equitably to assure the buyer that the items are being paid off. One method of accomplishing this would be to require that the payments be proportionate to the purchase price. For example, if a television set cost $200 and a chair cost $100, two-thirds of the monthly payment on the add-on contract would be applied to the television set and one-third to the chair. Items, as they were paid for in full, would no longer be subject to the contract. Surely, a seller should not be allowed to maintain equity in and control over merchandise that has actually been paid for.

Repossession

Our repossession laws must be amended to provide equal protection to the buyer. A repossession clause in a contract of a company in Washington, D. C., shows the appalling scope of the creditor's rights: ". . . in the event of a breach by the buyer of any provision herein contained, or in the event that the seller shall at any time deem itself or the goods, or any part thereof, for any reason, insecure, or unsafe, then in any such event the entire balance is due and owing under the terms and provisions of this agreement shall, at the option of the seller, be forthwith due and payable, and the seller shall have the right, with or without legal process, to retake the goods, no matter where they may be, and to retain them as its own property without obligation of resale, except as expressly provided by law, and without any duty to refund any part of the purchase price to the buyer and in such case do hereby waive and relinquish to and forever discharge said seller of and from all damages caused by entry or by such taking or removal of and from all claims by reason of such payments, entry, taking or removal. . . . The seller nevertheless shall have the right of resale for the account of the purchaser. In the event of a resale by the seller of the goods, or any part thereof, after a retaking, the proceeds of the resale shall be applied first to the payment of the expenses of retaking, keeping and reselling the goods, and then to the payment of the balance owing under this agreement; and if a deficiency results after such application, the buyer shall pay such deficiency."

Thus, we see that the seller can take back the merchandise if he believes it to be "insecure or unsafe," even though the purchaser faithfully keeps up payments. " 'Insecure' can mean the buyer is having domestic problems and the seller can repossess," says the former owner of a finance company. In many places the seller can repossess without any warning and by force. According to a judge in Texas, every debt-collection agency hires a crew to go out in the middle of the night and repossess cars off the street by breaking into them. "To repossess merchandise," reports an Ohio official, "creditors kick down doors, break windows, and even threaten to take people to jail if they resist. The victims are usually poor and don't know their rights."

We should outlaw arbitrary repossession, permitting repossession *only* when the buyer is in default, and we should forbid sellers from using strong-arm methods, like trespassing, breaking and entering, and using force in repossession. Such collection, if buyers will not voluntarily relinquish the merchandise, should be made through the legal process.

Our worst problem with repossession is the deficiency judgment, which is the amount the debtor must pay after he has returned the merchandise, it has been resold, and the resale price has been deducted from his original debt. The exploitation carried on in the name of deficiency judgments is notorious. "Extortion pure and simple," is what Lt. Col. Clyde Griffith, a judge advocate at Fort Myer, Virginia, called it before a House Banking and Currency Subcommittee in 1965. He described how soldiers were gouged by deficiency judgments. The soldier buys a used car for $600. Car insurance plus credit life insurance and finance charges raise the total price to $1,200. After paying $200 the soldier decides he cannot continue payments; the company repossesses the car and promptly sells it to a dummy bidder for $200, which is subtracted from the $1,000 debt. The soldier has no car, but still owes $800, much of it for two or three years of credit charges and insurance that he has never even used. The company resells the car at $600 again, packing it with $600 worth of finance charges. Such cars can be sold over and over, producing enormous incomes in credit charges, and are called "Lassies" because they always come home. The same racket was used to exploit the buyers of the stoves in Cleveland through the "garnishment ring." Some of these stoves were sold three and four times, as new, leaving a string of victims, all paying off $800 on the same stove.

Theoretically the repossessed merchandise is sold to help the debtor raise money to pay off his debt. The seller is supposed to try to obtain the highest possible price. In truth, the seller often sells the merchandise dirt-cheap to an accomplice. Under some circumstances public auctions are not required for the sale of repossessed merchandise; the debtor is not told that he himself can redeem the merchandise by purchasing it himself; in some instances the creditor himself can buy the repossessed goods at a *private sale*.

Sometimes the merchandise is quickly repossessed. One man in the District of Columbia had his car repossessed within a week; he was left with an $800 deficiency judgment. In Chicago, a man whose used car was repossessed still had to pay 142 percent of the cash price. Other times the unscrupulous seller waits until the merchandise is nearly paid off before he takes it back. In any event, he ends up with both the merchandise and the full price, and the consumer ends up with nothing, although he has paid hundreds of dollars.

We all know that merchandise, especially a new car, depreciates in value after it is purchased. Within the first week a new car that cost $2,800 may drop in cash value to $2,200. Were a company to repossess this car, it would not bring enough at resale to recoup the loss. Therefore, the deficiency judgment does have a legitimate purpose: it assures the dealer that he will be *fairly* compensated, that he is entitled to the difference between the purchase price and the true market value should the buyer default. This we can agree with. But under present circumstances, some dealers are not being fairly compensated; they are being overcompensated. They are being reimbursed for far more than any true loss; they are in fact piling up enormous, unwarranted profits through deficiency judgments (mostly for unused credit charges) by using merchandise as bait. This situation is grossly unfair and is not in keeping with the intent of deficiency judgments.

First, it seems to me that when a buyer has paid at least one-half of the purchase price on a piece of merchandise, he should be considered its legal owner; and it should not be subject to repossession without a court order. At that time the judge could consider any temporary financial difficulties which had prevented regular payments. Second, we must bring the amount of deficiency judgments back into the realm of *fair* compensation for the dealer. In England, the courts will not uphold outrageous deficiency judgments. In refusing to enforce a 75 percent deficiency judgment in 1953, a judge declared that the amount was not a valid estimate of the damage caused to the seller by the buyer's breach of contract. Such a deficiency judgment, he insisted, was rather a penalty, "an extravagant and extortionate sum held *in terrorem* over the head of the [purchaser]," to force him to carry out the contract rather than to compensate the seller justly. The courts traditionally refuse to uphold penalty clauses in contracts. The maximum that the British law will allow to be collected on repossessed merchandise is *one-half* of the total price, including credit charges.

We should consider similar legislation, setting a maximum on the amount that could be extracted for repossessed merchandise. Additionally, one should not be made to pay for finance charges and insurance charges which he has not used. If a car, for example, is repossessed within six months, the buyer should not have to pay three years worth of finance charges as may be called for in the original contract. Such charges should be prorated for the six months in a manner giving just compensation to the dealer. Furthermore, the creditor should not be permitted to buy back the merchandise himself, and his failure to give sufficient notice to the purchaser of his right to redeem the merchandise should be cause for a cancellation of the debt.

Holder in Due Course

The single factor most responsible for consumer injustices is the holder in due course doctrine. A New Jersey judge called it "the mask behind which fraud hides." Finance companies can work hand in hand with fraudulent operators, and unless it can be proved that the finance company is a knowing party, it cannot be held responsible, and the consumer must pay the fraudulent debt regardless. As we have seen, many moneylenders do not even investigate the companies from whom they buy consumer paper. Some buy at such high discounts that it would seem apparent that something is amiss. All banks and finance companies have the option of buying such consumer contracts and notes with defenses or without. "With defenses" the lender can, in turn, sue the seller if the contract was induced through misrepresentations or fraud, but many lenders buy "without defenses" (no right to sue) because the paper is cheaper and because they know they are invulnerable under the law, making them an innocent third party.

Our financing institutions should no longer be allowed to evade completely all responsibility for consumer deception. At the very least, the holder in due course doctrine should be altered so that the purchaser is allowed (and is told so explicitly in the contract) fifteen days in which to notify the bank or finance company of any deception, fraud, or other irregularities or complaints regarding his credit purchase. By notifying the lender of his dissatisfaction within the time period, the consumer would then be entitled to assert in court the same defenses—that is, fraud, misrepresentation—against the bank or finance company as he could against the seller. The consumer, within the limits of the provision, would not have to pay off fraudulent debts as he does now; he could go to court and obtain a cancellation of the contract.

Recognizing, however, that some cases of fraud would not be discovered within the fifteen-day period and that many consumers, through ignorance, would not assert their rights during the time limit, we should also give serious consideration to eliminating holder in due course altogether in consumer credit transactions, thus holding the financing institutions as equally responsible as the sellers for their involvement in consumer deception.

Some lenders complain that they could not do business without the protection of holder in due course. This is nonsense. Several states, including California, Maryland, Massachusetts, and Vermont, have eliminated holder in due course protection on consumer sales, and finance companies are still extending credit. Outlawing holder in due course would shift the risks and responsibilities of doing business back to moneylending institutions, help obliterate the finance companies that cater almost exclusively to known fraudulent firms, and make it more difficult for fraudulent dealers to obtain the needed financing to carry on business.

All of these debt-collection reforms would bring debtor laws up-to-date by reestablishing a legal basis for fair bargaining and at long last free consumers from their bondage to practices that force them to pay unjust debts and subject them to exploitation. Such reforms, by allowing the consumer to escape entrapment, will also make the practice of deception much less lucrative and attractive.

There is no single solution to our consumer ills, just as there is no single cause. Realistic laws, vigorous enforcement, consumer education, especially among the poor, and an increased responsibility in the ethical business community are all vital to combating consumer deception. Curtailing the activities of the unscrupulous and rectifying wrongs if deception does occur demand an organized resistance against the exploiters, based on the humane, commonsense philosophy that in a society like ours there is no place for the trickery and deceit by which deceptive merchants can drain the economy, drive people into debt, steal their homes, force them onto welfare, and lay waste to their lives under the guise of "doing business."

The ghost of "caveat emptor," which pits buyer against seller in a malevolent relationship, should finally be laid to rest. It is no longer appropriate, is seriously damaging to society, and surely is not conducive to engendering the trust and confidence necessary in today's complex marketplace.

PART TWO

leave many products free of safety restrictions. There is, for example, no all-inclusive law—federal, state, or municipal—which requires that *all* products be even reasonably safe, although we do have laws that prohibit the sale of specific hazardous products. Nor do our laws set even the barest safety standards on thousands of potentially dangerous products that are widely used, such as power lawn mowers. On some products we have regulated, such as flammable fabrics, the standards are so low as to be extremely ineffective, as Mr. Hackes's experience shows.

In view of the fact that accidents constitute a major health problem, it seems to me a tragic oversight that we have neglected such an elementary preventive measure as imposing reasonable safety standards on all products capable of causing death and injury.

According to National Safety Council figures, 60,000 persons this year will be killed in nonvehicular accidents, and about nine million, other than motorists, will suffer disabling accidental injuries —some serious and disfiguring. For persons aged one through thirty-six, accidents are the number one cause of death. It is impossible to predict how many of these accidents will be fully or partially caused by a hazardous product; the National Safety Council only recently began to collect figures on product involvement.

We can, however, make a number of estimates from past experience. One hundred and forty thousand persons will be mangled or killed while operating power mowers, countless others by tools in the workshop. About 100,000 persons will be cut, disfigured, or fatally injured while walking through glass doors. Twelve thousand persons will die, and 150,000 will suffer excruciating pain and often lifelong scars from fires, resulting from a match or lighted cigarette dropped on flammable clothing or upholstery. At least 1,000 will be electrocuted and many more burned and injured by faulty electrical equipment. Babies will strangle in ill-designed cribs; children will be poisoned by household cleaning fluids; whole families will be asphyxiated by carbon monoxide from faulty heaters; youngsters will be cut, blinded, and killed by dangerously designed toys. The list could go on almost endlessly.

The obvious question at this point is to what extent do these accidents result from human negligence and to what extent from the product itself. How one answers that question depends to a great degree on philosophy. For years, accident prevention efforts have focused on the individual's responsibility for an accident, and only rarely on the culpability of the product he was using. If a man is electrocuted by a defective power drill, he is at fault for not grounding it. (Says Morris Kaplan, technical director of Consumers Union: "We warn a man not to use a drill while standing in a puddle, although conceivably we could design one he could use safely while sitting in a bathtub.") If a child with a frilly dress backs into a space heater and is engulfed in flame, few stop to consider that the dress fabric may have been needlessly flammable; we blame the mother for failing to watch her. If a youngster gets his hand caught in the wringer of a washing machine, again it is not the machine's faulty design that is to blame; it is his parents' negligence.

We have, persistently, stubbornly, and I think the accident figures show, foolishly, pinned our hopes for reducing the accident toll on the "educational" method alone: warning people to use a product safely while almost totally ignoring the greater potential for preventing misery—building safety into the product itself. No one could deny that there is a critical need for more educational efforts in accident prevention. But when the main thrust of our efforts is to save humans from injury and death, we cannot close our eyes to an obvious solution that will accomplish our declared purpose, probably with undreamed-of speed. To allow human suffering to continue when we *know* how to relieve it would be unaccountably irresponsible. A tiny miscalculation in judgment, a bit of ignorance, should not condemn a man to accidental death if humanity and technology can conceivably prevent it.

Products *should* be made as safely as we know how, within the bounds of practicality. And I am convinced that the American people share that point of view. We naturally assume that when American ingenuity invents a "better mousetrap," it is automatically adopted. It was evident during the automobile safety controversy in 1966, which resulted in safety devices for cars, that a great number of Americans were surprised to discover that auto safety devices patented as long ago as the 1930s had not been incorporated into automobiles.

Periodically, Congress has taken action in response to public demand for protection. In 1953, after the country had been shocked by deaths and burns from sweaters that went up like torches, we passed a Flammable Fabrics Act, outlawing such outrageously combustible materials. In 1956, Congress reacted to the pathetic problem of youngsters suffocating inside refrigerators by requiring that refrigerator doors be made so they can be opened from the inside. In 1960, we passed a Hazardous Substances Labeling Act, requiring stringent warnings on all hazardous household substances. In 1966 came the passage of the Automobile Safety Act mandating a number of safety devices on automobiles, after the public outcry, resulting from Congressional hearings and the revelations of safety critics, including Ralph Nader, author of the best-selling book *Unsafe At Any Speed*. That same year, we passed the Child Protective Act and later the Flammable Fabrics Amendments of 1967, the Child Protection and Toy Safety Act of 1969, and the Poison Prevention Packaging Act of 1970 which prohibits packaging poisonous substances in containers unnecessarily attractive to children.

Essential as these measures are, they still provide only an ineffective patchwork of safety. They still leave Americans totally unprotected from vast numbers of potentially injurious and deadly products. Moreover, such measures are born of indignation and tragedy. Predictably, unless we take a reasoned look at the whole spectrum of hazardous products, there will be more tragedies and more indignation, as the horror of another accident "epidemic" is uncovered. Is this really the most sensible way to handle such a life and death problem? Why can we not ferret out and correct the hazards in products *before* they cause injuries and death? After-the-fact protection is of little consolation to the millions who have already suffered. As I recently observed in the Senate: "If there is ever a situation in which hindsight outshines foresight it is in the field of accident prevention." It is time that we reverse the direction of our vision.

Unquestionably, there are unsafe products on the market. In its final report presented in June 1970, after intensive surveys and hearings, the National Commission on Product Safety thoroughly documented how dozens of products can injure and kill. Among them are glass doors, color television sets, fireworks, floor furnaces, exploding glass soft-drink bottles, bicycles with "high-rise" handlebars, hot-water vaporizers, household chemicals, infant furniture, ladders, power tools, rotary lawn mowers, toys, unvented gas heaters, wringer washing machines, electric blankets, lead paint, flammable eyeglass frames, aerosol containers, cosmetics.

Some excerpts from the Commission's report:

"*Architectural glass.* One parent whose child survived a collision with a glass door testified: 'I heard a tremendous loud crashing of glass and some horrible screams. . . . The screams intensified and I turned around and looked at the entranceway where I saw a number of neighbors and they began to scream. So I ran to the entranceway and as I got about halfway there, I saw my son . . . on his hands and knees. Immediately above him was a jagged piece of glass which had remained in its casing. And it started to slide down in the fashion that a guillotine would with the exception that the glass was jagged and pointed directly at his head. I was approximately fifteen feet away when I saw this, and I just hoped that I would get there before the glass did. As I looked at him, he was a mass of blood and there was glass falling all about him, and, of course, he was screaming. Luckily I did get there and I got my right hand above his neck and the glass stopped approximately two inches above his neck.'

"*Color television sets.* On New Year's Day, 1966, the Fassero family of Springfield, Illinois, after a day of watching TV programs in color, turned off the set and went to bed. During the night, Mr. Fassero found the living room in flames, attributed to a fire in the TV set. The house was gutted. Mrs. Fassero was disabled. Her mother died of the effects of the fire. . . . Among the 85 million TV sets in the United States in 1969 including about 20 million color sets, about 10,000 sets caught on fire. Most of the fires were in color sets.

"*Floor furnaces.* 'The temperature at the level of the floor grate has been recorded at between 300° and 350° F, the usual temperature for cooking chicken, beef, ham, veal and other meats,' Dr. Julian A. Waller, professor at the University of Vermont Medical School told us in February, 1969. 'The only other heating device so constructed is the barbecue.' . . . Gas-fired floor furnaces have been searing infant flesh and imprinting waffle-pattern scars for years. The metal grille of a floor furnace includes a crisscross cover. Contact with the skin at a temperature of approximately 155° F for one second will produce second-degree burns. At 300° to 350° the burn is instantaneous and often permanently disfiguring.

"*Glass bottles.* 'I will be blind in one eye for the rest of my life because of a defective glass bottle.' The testimony of fourteen-year-old Sharon Jackson of Chicago tells the tragic potential of exploding glass bottles. . . . Although explosions are the most dramatic cause of injury from glass bottles, they are not the most common. Insurance companies reported more claims related to glass bottles than to any other consumer product.

"*High-rise bicycles.* At our first hearing in New York City, Dr. Allan B. Coleman, chairman of the American Academy of Pediatrics Committee on Accident Prevention, voiced alarm over hazards associated with new bicycle designs. He stated: 'The currently popular bicycles with high-rise handlebars are causing undue numbers of cheek injuries. . . .'

"*Hot-water vaporizers.* The McCormack family bought a Hankscraft vaporizer advertised as tipproof, foolproof, and safe. It bore the seals of *Good Housekeeping* and *Parents'* magazines, and the mark of Underwriters' Laboratories. They placed it on a stool in their home, plugged it in the house circuit, and waited for the steam to rise. While it was steaming, their three-year-old daughter caught herself in its electric cord. The vaporizer tipped and spilled scalding water onto the child. Andrea McCormack spent five months in the hospital enduring a series of painful operations. She will bear the scars all her life. . . .

"*Infant furniture.* 'I would never want anyone else to be put through the pain and grief which we had and still always will have. It was a horrible nightmare.' This letter from a mother whose infant son was strangled by the top of his own crib unfortunately was not unique. Although we have reliable reports of deaths linked to the product of one manufacturer, the design of nearly identical crib models on the market suggests that others also may be culpable. In Dade County, Florida, alone, crib slats, sides or tops have strangled at least one infant every year for the past ten years. Nationwide as many as 200 deaths each year may be laid to crib strangulations. Near misses are not uncommon."

Even a cursory examination of a few products reveals that simple design changes could eliminate a number of accidents. In some instances the design improvement is so simple and inexpensive that it is tragic it was not required years ago. A classic case of neglect is the wringer washing machine.

Contrary to what most of us may think, the wringer washer is still very much a part of the American scene. Millions of them are still in use, mainly in lower economic areas, and 379,000 new ones were sold in 1968. Every year, about 100,000 children and an equal number of adults undergo the horror of seeing their hands, fingers, arms, and clothing being caught and fed through the turning rollers. Many injuries are minor—bruises and lacerations. Many others—one in six, estimates one doctor—are "crushing injuries to the soft tissues and muscle, erosion of the superficial and deep structures of the skin, fractures of the bones, and occasional fatalities." Many injuries result in massive swelling and lifelong scars; and the emotional trauma to child-victims is immeasurable, say doctors.

Yet, since the late 1940s, the manufacturers of wringer washing machines have had available to them a simple "instinctive" safety release which would virtually eliminate these cruel injuries. A youngster rarely is tall enough, strong enough, or has the presence of mind to operate the old-fashioned bar or lever on the sides of the wringer, which require a considerable blow before the rollers separate. With the instinctive release, a tug of a mere fifteen pounds, as the child "instinctively" tries to withdraw his hand, causes the rollers to stop and come apart. The cost to the manufacturer for such a safety device is five dollars. Considering the small cost of the device and the magnitude of the problem, it is appalling then to discover that in 1969, about 47 percent of all new wringer washing machines in retail stores did *not* possess this release.

At the urging of doctors, Underwriters' Laboratories in 1968 finally adopted a new standard requiring that wringer washers be equipped either with an instinctive release or a "dead man's" release, in which the rollers stop when the operator takes his foot off an electric switch in a footpad. UL's standard was far overdue and welcome, although it is merely voluntary and cannot be legally enforced. And the standard does not take care of the millions of hazardous wringer washers that are expected to last for twenty to twenty-five years. Unless an adapter can be found to convert these machines, wringer arm injuries will persist for many years.

Another case in point is the glass in patio doors, storm doors, and shower doors. Much of the glass installed in sliding glass doors is only three-sixteenths of an inch thick, about twice the thickness of an ordinary windowpane. Every year, according to U. S. Public Health Service biostatisticians, about 100,000 persons are injured, some fatally, from walking or running into these doors, which appear to be open.

As early as 1961, safety officials pointed out that such injuries were needless, that they could be prevented by the use of safety glass in the doors. The extra cost to the consumer for tempered glass in a typical six-foot sliding glass door is but $10 to $13, in a storm door, $5 to $7. Recent publicity about the hazard brought forth laws in twenty-two states requiring safety glazing on doors. But twenty-eight states still lack such laws. Annually, more than a million sliding glass doors are put into new construction and remodeled buildings. Despite vigorous campaigns for safety glass by the Architectural Aluminum Manufacturers Association and by public health and safety officials, many contractors are reportedly still installing some patio doors and many storm doors of highly dangerous glass.

Similarly, it seems apparent that all shower doors, where a person is particularly vulnerable to slipping, should be made of safety glass or plastic. Yet, a woman in Chicago wrote me recently that when she ordered a safety-glass shower enclosure for a remodeled home, it was a special order and took ten weeks to arrive.

No single household product holds such potential for human destruction as the power lawn mower, notably the rotary mower with its whirling blade that can amputate fingers, toes, hands, and feet; and hurl wire, rocks, glass, nails, and all manner of debris at speeds approaching that of a bullet. So fantastic is the force that bits of wire have been driven completely through the skull and fragments of glass have penetrated the heart.

Our defenses against this machine are severely limited. We are told to "get people, especially children, out of the way when mowing." Some objects, however, are hurled long distances, through windows and into neighbors' yards. One little boy was struck unconscious by a rock that was hurled fifty-five feet by a mower. In another instance a stick thrown by a mower went through the open window of a passing car, puncturing the eye of a passenger.

Eliminating such injuries by "properly cleaning the lawn before mowing," as we are instructed to do, is not entirely practicable. A quick tour of the lawn to check for debris might be a reasonable precaution; but it seems to me if one has to go over an entire lawn to remove every small stone and two-inch piece of wire that might be embedded in the grass, one might as well cut the lawn with scissors.

The caveat "always wear shoes when using a power mower" seems sensible enough, but is of little value when the high-horsepower engines rotate the blades at speeds great enough to slice through leather. One man had all the toes of his right foot amputated when he pulled a mower over his heavy engineering boot; the blade neatly sliced through the boot at mid-foot, severing a leather sole an inch thick.

For years we have been warned to turn off the motor when adjusting the blade or leaving the mower. Yet, thousands of children are maimed by getting caught in mowers left unattended, and thousands of adults have their fingers amputated when trying to remove grass and other debris from the housing while the blades are whirling.

Obviously then, with 80,000 Americans being hideously injured by these mowers every year, our futile efforts at education are no substitute for drastically needed safety improvements in the mower itself. In 1965, the University of Iowa's Institute of Agricultural Medicine noted in its study of power mower accidents: "The power mower that can perform with ease, power, and optimum safety has yet to be put on the market. . . . Today's machine is potentially as dangerous as the first model."

It seems incredible that in all these years (the rotary mower came into popular use soon after World War II), American ingenuity has not been able to devise some method to confine dangerous objects within the mower's housing. L. W. Knapp, Jr., director of the University of Iowa's power mower study, says tests confirm that the lower the housing, the less the threat of expelled objects, and that "closing the housing clearance at the rear of the mower [perhaps by some sort of dragging apron] would stop the expulsion of objects to the rear altogether." The discharge chute on some mowers is angled toward the rear, making the operator a direct target for expelled objects. Some discharge chutes are aimed at an undesirably high angle, shooting projectiles out in high arcs, when a lower angle would tend to send them skittering harmlessly across the ground. Riding mowers are notoriously unstable; many have toppled over, trapping their occupants underneath. Moreover, few riding mowers have leakproof gasoline caps (which cost about two cents extra); thus, in case of tippage, gas could drop down onto the hot manifold and ignite. Additionally, controls on the mowers are not uniform; on one mower the brake may be on the left, on another, on the right.

Blades can undoubtedly be made safer. Said the Iowa report: "The blade should be designed to stop automatically any time the operator releases the handle or leaves the seat," just as an automatic clothes dryer stops when the door is opened. Investigators also noted that the high speeds of the blade are unnecessary. Tests show that the blade cuts grass just as well at 11,000 feet per minute as at the commonly used 19,000 feet per minute. A reduction in the blade speed would reduce the force with which objects are hurled and lessen the blade's ability to cut through protective clothing and tissue.

Recently, power mower manufacturers have become increasingly aware of the need to improve the safety of their mowers. The Outdoor Power Equipment Institute, Inc., a trade association which includes those companies manufacturing 86 percent of the power mowers in the country, has made commendable efforts to upgrade the design of mowers by sponsoring research, setting higher safety standards for members to follow, and granting a "safety seal" to be used on all mowers meeting the standards. However, a survey by the National Commission on Product Safety in 1969 revealed that only one-quarter of 216 models examined met industry's own safety specifications. And some manufacturers affixed OPEI's seal without meeting standards. OPEI, being a voluntary organization, has no means of policing members.

"For at least ten years prior to our hearings, manufacturers were aware of the dangers attendant to high surface temperatures of floor furnaces," reported the National Commission on Product Safety. (There are approximately two million gas-fired floor furnaces in the United States.) "Yet in February 1969, more than 10 years after the industry had been put on notice, the voluntary industry standard stipulated grille temperatures not to exceed 350° above room temperature, or about 420°. During that interval 300,000 persons—many of them children—suffered floor furnace burns severe enough to require medical treatment."

"On short notice and for a modest fee," the Commission asked Weiner Associates, Inc. to devise methods of protecting persons from floor grille burns without impairing use of the furnace. They came up with three possible solutions:

1. A finned-aluminum grille radiator
2. An evaporatively cooled grille radiator
3. An insulated silastic rubber impregnated into a fiberglass matrix.

All of these proposals, according to the Commission, would either reduce the grille temperature below 120° or insulate against higher temperatures at a modest cost.

Preventing electrical shock also has not been approached from the most practical point of view. Traditionally, we are told to avoid shock by "grounding the tool and not using electrical equipment around water." Grounding portable tools is undependable on two-wire systems and most homes do not have three-hole outlets to accommodate the third grounding wire on new tools. A better solution is double insulation, in which the manufacturer encloses the shock-producing interior of the product in two layers of insulation instead of the usual one. If the regular insulation breaks down, there is a second line of defense to prevent current leakage. Portable drills, hedge clippers, lawn mowers, sanders, saws, floor scrubbers, can be made with double insulation.

A surprising number of household appliances leak excessive current, enough to give a significant jolt. Morris Kaplan of CU points out that the threat of shock on some appliances could be eliminated by repositioning a component or by inserting an insulating washer between the component and the metal parts that extend to the outside casing. In old-fashioned ceiling lights, operated by a pull chain, one wooden insulating link was inserted midway in the metal chain to prevent a wayward current from coursing the full length of the chain. The same principle could be applied to appliances, such as radios. The cost of the insulating washers: about one-fourth of a cent apiece.

On a moment's reflection, one could suggest dozens of design improvements to prevent accidents. One—safety closures on household substances which have caused many accidental poisonings to children—recently was made a legal requirement under the Poison Prevention Packaging Act in December 1970. The Food and Drug Administration at the time of this writing has recommended "childproof" containers for aspirin and furniture oil polishes containing 10 percent or more petroleum distillates. FDA, with the advice of an eighteen-member Technical Advisory Committee, will periodically recommend childproof packaging for other products found to cause high numbers of poisonings. Other design improvements include:

The elimination of sharp edges on children's toys and the routine use of painted or felt eyes on stuffed toys instead of the old-fashioned "harpoon" eyes, which are simply stuck in the toy with a long pin or sharp piece of metal.

Narrower spaces between the slats in babies' playpens and cribs so it is impossible for the baby to wedge his head through the openings.

Outside air vents on all heaters intended for use indoors; some heaters come without vents on them and have caused carbon monoxide poisoning.

The removal of the hard, brittle plastic steering wheels from children's car seats, or their replacement by soft plastic. In accidents, the hard plastic often shatters and cuts a child's face.

Curl-up cords on electric coffee pots, instead of the long dangling ones that youngsters can grab, tipping the scalding liquid onto themselves.

Eyeglasses with nonflammable frames. Some frames made of cellulose nitrate literally explode in flames. One man, as he lit a cigar, suffered facial burns when the frame of his glasses "went up like a rag soaked in gasoline."

The possibilities are many. But nowhere is the need for upgrading safety standards more critical than in the flammability of fabrics.

About one million persons, according to the U.S. Public Health Service, suffer burn injuries every year, and estimates indicate that flammable clothing is implicated in about 150,000 of these burns. In addition, of the 6,000 persons who die every year in home fires —2,000 of them children—an inestimable number are victims of poisonous smoke produced by combustible interior furnishings that "feed the fire."

Few people appreciate how flammable ordinary clothing fabrics are. It is not an exotic cloth that is most often implicated in clothing-fire burns, but most often plain ordinary cotton. An analysis by the Academy of Pediatrics in 1964 revealed a situation that still exists: that of clothing-fire burns, fully 75 percent were due to the ignition of cotton and rayon. Partly accountable for this fact is that cotton is our most widely used fabric. However, through tests, the study also confirmed what is generally unappreciated among the public: that cotton is also the *fastest burning* fabric in common use. Samples of the clothing causing the burns were collected by the academy and ignited. Cotton went up the fastest: one swatch ignited in one second, as compared with seven seconds required to light a sample from a wool sweater. (Wool, in fact, is our slowest burning natural fiber.) Synthetics, such as dacron and nylon, were also harder to ignite and slower to burn than cotton. In summary, the academy reported:

"Although most persons believe new synthetics are more flammable than cotton, the opposite is generally true. Rayon is not any more flammable than cotton, while all other synthetics are less flammable and some will hardly burn at all."

This does not mean, however, that synthetics are incapable of producing burns. Some nylons often melt and stick to the skin like molten lava, giving deep penetrating burns long after the flame has been extinguished.

Most of us have an abiding faith in the miracles of modern medicine: the belief that if the burns are not prevented, at least they can be healed. Thus, it is sobering indeed to hear the grim prognostications by many doctors about clothing-fire injuries. Burns are considered our most difficult injury to treat. During the hearings to amend the Flammable Fabrics Act, Dr. Abraham B. Bergman, director of the Outpatient Services at the Children's Orthopedic Hospital and Medical Center in Seattle, told of the medical profession's helplessness in treating burn victims:

"The treatment of burns remains completely unsatisfactory despite advances in other fields of medicine. We haven't materially improved the survival rate in over thirty years, nor have we done much to alter morbidity. The best plastic surgery still leaves terrible scars. Our modern treatment of shock has merely meant that patients die three weeks after their burn rather than three days. Perhaps we can save an occasional life by some treatment methods that have recently come on the scene—but there is little hope on the horizon that medical science will materially alter this grim picture."

Dr. Bergman told of a typical tragedy: "Three weeks ago in Richmond, Washington, a little 2½-year-old girl, Suzanne, was playing in the living room with an older sister. The sister rushed into her parents' bedroom crying, 'Suzy's on fire!' Indeed she was! When her mother reached Suzy, she was a human torch. It was the all-too-familiar story. She was wearing a flannel nightgown, and there was a space heater in the room. She sustained full thickness burns (third degree) over 85 percent of her body. The only areas spared were her lower legs and feet. I have pictures of Suzy here with me, but have elected not to show them to you—there is no point. I didn't even have the heart to take my medical students into the room last week, because she looked so horrible.

"It was apparent from the moment we saw Suzy that she must inevitably die—the question was only how long it would take. In cases such as this I earnestly pray that the end comes sooner, rather than later. I spoke with the parents every day, attempting to comfort them and prepare them for the outcome. Understandably [the father], a patrolman in a small town, and his wife had a difficult time accepting this. What finally seemed to help was their eventual realization that were a miracle to ensue, her life, after surviving such a severe burn, would be worse than death.

"In all honesty I must say that I do not consider it a triumph when the life of a severely burned child is saved. A lifetime of operations, pain, disfigurement, scarring, and rejection by society and self lie ahead. Death may be more merciful."

Over and over, doctors see these hopeless cases: Margot, four and a half, whose nightgown sleeve caught fire while she played with a cigarette lighter, had her entire right arm and right side of her face permanently scarred; Ronnie, three, who stretched his arm over a stove burner, igniting his flannel pajamas, suffered burns over 70 percent of his body; Lynda, a beautiful teen-age girl, who will never be beautiful again, had the edge of her frilly nightgown caught by a space heater and she ran, fanning the flames; a woman, eighty-three, attempting to cook for herself, brushed the sleeve of her cotton dress over a burner and was fatally burned; a man in his seventies, confined to a wheelchair, accidentally ignited his shirt while smoking and was helpless to rescue himself. An estimated 55 percent of all clothing fires happen to youngsters under nine and to those over seventy-five.

Dr. Bergman tells of a boy now eighteen, who has been in the hospital thirteen separate times for a total of 130 days since he was burned at age fourteen months when his clothing brushed against a stove, burning him over 60 percent of his body. The boy quit school at age twelve because of his appearance and for the last four years has been a ward of the juvenile court. Another boy, sixteen, was severely burned at age four, failed in school, and is under psychiatric care after being arrested for indecent exposure.

Not only are the human costs intolerable, but the costs of attempting to treat burn patients are astronomical. The cost for treating an acute burn patient runs about $100 a day, and the victim usually must remain hospitalized for months, with periodic returns. It is not unusual for a bill for the treatment of one burned youngster to reach $30,000. The cost of many victims' treatment must be absorbed by public funds.

Is not this problem of clothing burns another dramatic example of our backward approach to accident prevention? We cry for more doctors to treat burned patients, more hospital facilities, more public funds, more medical research—all to alleviate this mountain of human suffering and waste, when right now we could take positive steps to *prevent* it by insisting on the use of fabric that does not turn youngsters' clothing into fiery torches.

Safety messages on the dangers of clothing fires must sound hollow indeed to parents whose children have been killed or disfigured by burning clothing. As Dr. Bergman said: "I believe accidents will always be with us, and it doesn't do much good to be morally indignant about how they occur, particularly when they involve children. . . . Surely we must increase our efforts in safety education, but not use calls for safety education, which cost little and hurt no one, as a rapier to fend off action which will be more effective in achieving the end result. . . . What is needed to prevent serious burn injuries is clothing which does not readily support combustion."

The outcry against flammable fabrics is hardly new. In 1861, after the wife of Henry Wadsworth Longfellow was burned to death when her muslin dress caught fire, *Scientific American* magazine urged "the preparation of ladies' dresses with nonflammable material." More than one hundred years later, however, clothing of noncombustible fabrics is still not generally available to the public, although many such fabrics are technologically possible. Certain types of cotton materials can be successfully treated with chemicals to make them noncombustible. A number of synthetic fabrics have been created which because of their chemical composition are nearly impossible to ignite: for example, Dynel, developed by Union Carbide Corp.; Verel, from Eastman Chemical Products, Inc.; Nomex, by DuPont; fiberglass, made by several companies.

A demonstration before our consumer subcommittee by William V. White, now director, Division of Consumer Product Safety, FDA, dramatically showed the life-saving properties of these fabrics. Mr. White produced two swatches of white cotton, one treated and one untreated. He touched a match flame to the ordinary cotton; it caught fire instantly and was quickly consumed in flame. (I am convinced that the average person would be more than a little enlightened to see how readily and brightly cotton shoots up in flame.) Mr. White then applied a flame to the cotton swatch which had been commercially impregnated with a fire-retardant chemical called THPC. Although he held the flame to a corner of the cotton for several seconds, it would not ignite; the only sign of flame damage was a slight charring.

The chemical THPC treatment was developed nineteen years ago, in 1953, at the U. S. Department of Agriculture's Southern Regional Research Laboratory in New Orleans. It is true that this chemical additive is not the final answer for rendering *all* cottons flame-retardant. For, although there is no question of the treated cotton's durability (it will withstand 75 to 100 washings without losing its flame-retardancy), the treatment does result in a slight harshness and stiffness and added weight to the fabric, making it unsuitable for use in garments where softness and light weight are desired. The treatment also causes white cotton when bleached to turn slightly yellow.

In an attempt to overcome these objections, the USDA's Laboratory has developed a variation of the treatment, called THPOH. In September 1967, USDA researchers announced that with the THPOH formula, lightweight cotton fabrics can be treated without "an appreciable difference in hand." ("We have treated cotton fabrics as light weight as that in an Indian sari without a significant change in hand," says George Drake, head of USDA's special finishes investigation.) However, some weight is added by the new treatment—about 16 percent on gingham and 13 percent on sateen. There is no yellowing of the treated fabric during bleaching.

Additionally, the American Viscose Division of FMC Corporation has developed a fire-retardant treatment in which a phosphate chemical is injected into rayon fiber at the time it is manufactured. Since this results in a chemical displacement instead of a chemical add-on, the treatment causes no change in weight or hand of the material and thus could be used in all garments, even the most frilly. The Ciba Chemical and Dye Company, too, among other companies, has developed a new chemical treatment for nonflammable cotton which reportedly is extremely successful.

It is apparent that more research in the laboratories and testing in the mills are needed before the process of flame-retardancy for cotton is perfected, and all cotton garments can be made noncombustible on a wide commercial scale. Nevertheless THPC-treated cloth right now is suitable for heavy and medium weight cotton items. Army fliers in Vietnam are wearing suits of fire-retardant cotton. So are workers in steel mills, where molten metal could ignite clothing. Sears Roebuck and Co. offers sweat shirts made fire-safe with THPC. A number of articles of clothing—dresses, pajamas, robes—have been made up for children, as experimental models in this country. And in England, now, children are wearing cotton sleepwear—robes, pajamas, gowns—treated with Proban, a THPC process. Since October 1964, Great Britain has required by law that all sleeping garments designed to be sold to youngsters under age thirteen be fire-retardant. In addition, THPC flame-retardant draperies and cubicle curtains are being used in hospitals and nursing homes here and abroad. That we are not able to buy more items made from these lifesaving materials is regrettable. The extra retail cost of treated cotton items is about 20 percent and would be lower under mass production.

In his demonstration, Mr. White also proved with the match test that a number of the new synthetic fabrics will not readily support combustion, or even char.

Racing car drivers and the U. S. Forestry Department's smoke-jumpers who parachute into forest fires are wearing suits of flame-proof Nomex. Verel is found in coats, slippers, carpets, and rugs. After the tragic deaths of the three astronauts in the space capsule fire, suits for astronauts are now being made from fireproof fiberglass.

Too little attention has been given to the role of flammable fabrics in spreading fire and causing death from smoke inhalation. We know that a fire in a home must have something to feed on or it would go out; normally, that fuel is flammable draperies, carpeting, chair coverings, beddings, and especially mattresses. The absence of combustible interior furnishings would prevent many fires. In addition, countless lives would be saved by the use of nonflammable fabrics for upholstery and bedding.

It is not generally known that the real killer in a home fire is not the flames, but poisonous smoke, produced by the burning combustibles. Actually, many of the dead are carried out of a fire without a burn on their bodies; according to some indications as many as 80 percent of all persons who die in fires are asphyxiated by poisonous smoke. Tests have shown that burning interior furnishings can give off at least a dozen poisonous gases, including carbon monoxide, hydrocyanic acid, hydrogen sulfide, ammonia, and phosgene.

The number one home fire hazard is smoking, causing an estimated 200,000 fires annually and the loss of 1,200 lives. A dropped cigarette burns through upholstery or a mattress and smolders in the stuffing, sometimes for hours, producing streams of odorless, invisible poisonous gases, before bursting into flame. Tests conducted by the Los Angeles Fire Department revealed that a smoldering chair will fill a room with a knockout concentration of carbon monoxide within an hour, without raising the temperature above a comfortable 70 degrees.

In such fires, the victims die quietly, often in their sleep. Not long ago in Michigan, firemen found a man and his wife and two children in their upstairs bedrooms, lying peacefully in their beds. All four had been asphyxiated by a fire that had started downstairs in the den and never spread from that room. A smoldering couch, ignited by a cigarette, had given off lethal gases which had risen silently, flooding the top floors of the house.

This tragedy would not have occurred if the couch had been covered with a fire-retardant fabric to prevent the cigarette from burning through into the stuffing.

Fireproof draperies, pillows, bedspreads, upholstery, carpeting—of fiberglass or other nonburn synthetics and of all patterns and prices (draperies from $4.98 to custom-made $400)—are now available in some stores. Dealers, however, have been reluctant to advertise this lifesaving property, under the old theory that "safety doesn't sell," and shoppers have a difficult time even finding a label indicating an item is "fireproof." Dealers and manufacturers would do a public service by pointing up these safety features, and, indeed, Owens Corning Fiberglass Corporation does have a multimillion-dollar advertising campaign to publicize the fire-retardant qualities of their products.

Unquestionably, certain fire-retardant fabrics are available which can and should be used to stop these tragic accidents from fires—if not at the initiative of industry, then at the insistence of government. We now have the legislation, in the Flammable Fabrics Act as amended in 1967, to enable us to set higher minimum standards of flammability for all fabrics. The original Flammable Fabrics Act, which was passed in 1953 in response to a number of tragedies from "torch" sweaters, was inadequate and, in some ways, gave the public a false sense of security.

Under this law, we were able to outlaw only the most outrageously flammable fabrics in wearing apparel, such as the brushed rayon "torch" sweaters which were completely consumed by flame in twenty to forty seconds. Such articles of clothing as hats, gloves, and babies' receiving blankets were not included under the law. Nor did the definition of the term "fabric" under the law extend to upholstery materials, draperies, carpeting, sheets, and blankets. Thus, while we were able to outlaw "torch" sweaters, we were helpless to protect the public from the estimated four million "torch" blankets, made from the identical brushed rayon, which are sold yearly to cover people while they sleep. A few years ago, the Chicago Fire Commissioner ran a series of tests on these blankets, made of 88 percent rayon and 12 percent acrylic and widely sold in Chicago retail stores. A split second after a flame was touched to the blanket's edge, it became a mass of flames and was completely consumed in four seconds.

It was Congress's intent that the standards established by the 1953 Flammable Fabrics Act would be gradually stiffened in subsequent years. Yet, when our consumer subcommittee of the Senate Commerce Committee held hearings on updating the act in May 1967, I discovered that the committee to draw up tougher standards *had not met for ten years.*

The 1953 Flammable Fabrics Act, which was imperative at the time and was a piece of legislation I firmly supported, on reflection proved to be an inflexible, narrow approach to accident prevention, which appears to have actually stifled progress and frozen standards at a low level. The act illustrates the inadvisability of passing legislation to deal with a specific emergency in after-the-fact fashion. Our whole philosophy of safety legislation, instead, should be anticipatory and comprehensive. We should not wait until tragedy is upon us. We should study the potential hazards in a reasoned atmosphere and take precautionary measures *before* an epidemic of accidents occurs.

Toward that objective of prevention instead of panic-action, Congress in 1967 accepted my suggestions for amending the Flammable Fabrics Act. The amendments provide a flexible, continuing program for detecting flammable fabric hazards and for taking action to reduce them before they cause more deaths and injuries and become a subject of national outrage. Under the amendments, the Secretary of Commerce is authorized to conduct research into flammable fabrics; the Secretary of Health, Education and Welfare is directed to investigate continually deaths and injuries from accidental burns; and the Secretary of Commerce, drawing on his own and HEW's investigations and all other available information, is authorized to set flammability standards for fabrics when he discovers that such action is needed to protect the public from harm. Furthermore, the law is extended to cover not only clothing fabrics, but *all* fabrics, including those used in interior furnishings, such as bedding, draperies, carpets, upholstery, and any other conceivable product that could be created in the future.

However, four years later we can say that the Department of Commerce's performance in setting such standards has been highly disappointing, characterized by delay and a favoritism toward industry at the cost of burned and scarred children. Standards have not yet been set for many items: blankets, upholstery, mattresses. On such items, the extra cost of making coverings fire-resistant to prevent cigarettes from burning through to the stuffing would be insignificant or nonexistent. Flameproof synthetics are no more expensive and are often cheaper than more flammable fabrics. Such upholstery for overstuffed furniture—and most assuredly mattress ticking—should be routinely fireproofed.

The National Bureau of Standards, part of the Commerce Department, did set flammability standards for carpets, effective January 1972, but they are so weak as hardly to represent a significant change. Carpets which are highly flammable can still meet the standard.

Even more shameful is the action, or lack of it, on fire-retardant fabrics for children's clothing which allows such pain and human destruction. Finally, after four years, Commerce announced fire-resistant requirements for children's *sleepwear only,* up to size 6X *only,* and gave manufacturers two years grace period, until July 1973, to comply!

For far too long we have abdicated our responsibility for preserving life in the nebulous hope that safe products will emerge full-blown from conscience or competition within the business community. This is unrealistic. Such are competitive pressures that instead of promoting safety, our present quality of competition often militates against it. Safety is often not seen as a profitable commodity when pitted against styling, ease of operation, and cost. When asked why they had not incorporated the $2 instinctive release on their wringer washing machine, one company admitted that even such a small expenditure that would require some alterations in production would require a higher price, giving competitors an edge in a low-income market, where every dollar off counts. Competition did not bring us the livesaving devices on automobiles, such as the collapsible steering wheel, recessed instrument panels, disc brakes.

Recently, an automotive engineer told me that many in the auto industry were secretly glad that a law was passed, mandating the use of the safety features by all companies, for competition had long prevented their adoption by one company alone.

The threat of lawsuits, ending in large personal injury settlements, reputedly spurs industry to develop safer products, and undoubtedly this is true to some extent. But Arnold Elkind, noted personal injury attorney in New York City, predicts that as the judgments become more common, some companies, instead of improving their product, will increase their insurance coverage and pass the extra cost for the premiums on to the consumer. Moreover, sacrificing humans in the hope that eventually their suffering will have some meaning for the rest of society seems to me, at the very least, a primitive approach to product improvement.

Industry, also, through a number of scientific and technical committees, trade associations, and the American National Standards Institute (ANSI), formulates uniform safety standards for products. Although such industry standards serve a useful purpose, they cannot be depended upon to guarantee us the safest products possible. The standards subscribed to by industry do not represent the greatest safety achievement possible; on the contrary, the standards are adopted by consensus and thus represent the lowest common denominator, the level at which nearly all the membership is willing to comply. Although the new ANSI claims to be reconstituted to consider consumer opinion, the consumer ordinarily has little real voice in determining the standards. Consumers Union, a member of ANSI, reports that its suggestions have consistently been voted down, overwhelmed by the "consensus" of industry.

Coming to the "consensus" is a slow, tedious process and is often of little immediate benefit to the consumer. In response to the outcry over glass door accidents, an ANSI committee worked for nearly four years to develop an acceptable standard for the performance of safety glass and how to test it. The standard, however, does not specify that safety glass must be used—only that if it is used, it meet certain criteria. It is then up to the individual companies and trade associations of the industry affected to decide whether they wish to comply with the standard. In this instance, the Architectural Aluminum Manufacturers Association, a trade association for the makers of sliding glass doors, has required that its member companies use safety glass in all sliding doors as of June 30, 1968.

Not all companies, of course, subscribe to the agreed-on standards, and as we know, the companies that most need to improve their products are the least likely to belong to such groups. Nor, even within the membership of the standard-setting group, can the use of the standards be enforced, as was strikingly illustrated by the OPEI members who used the ANSI safety seal on substandard mowers.

Once a standard is adopted by industry, it also seems to freeze and take on elevated importance, ascending from the position of "consensus" to the epitome of the possible. Compliance with industry standards, for example, is used in lawsuits as evidence that a product was not negligently designed because the design was agreed-on industry-wide. Government standards, too, that are set too low, actually militate against product improvement. Many lawyers have been defeated in attempting to prove an article of clothing excessively flammable because the manufacturer can show that it met government requirements and therefore must be safe.

Clearly, the consumer now is afforded only hit-and-miss protection against hazardous products, dependent upon an incoherent patchwork of voluntary industry standards, the possible threat to manufacturers of large personal injury settlements, and a scattering of laws pertaining to specific products.

It is evident that we need a tough, effective omnibus consumer product safety law—backed up by tough enforcers—to bring under control the many hazards associated with products. To study the problem, Congress, at our request established a National Commission on Product Safety in 1967. It was to investigate the nature and scope of product hazards, the effectiveness of present legislation and industry standards. The Commission's final report was issued in 1970 after two years of work in which it collected impressive data—through staff investigations and public hearings—pointing up the need for such an omnibus law.

In addition to adequate enforcement powers, we need, in my opinion, a federal Omnibus Consumer Product Safety Agency that would consolidate all our concerns about the safety of foods, drugs, and other consumer products under one federal roof. Such an agency, comprised of a Commission of Food Safety, a Commission of Drug Safety and a Commission of Product Safety, would be charged with "promoting public health by protecting consumers against death, injury, or illness from foods, drugs and other consumer products."

Such an agency, among other duties, would set safety standards, collect and analyze data on injuries and deaths from consumer products, take action against violators, and demand recall of unsafe items. To prevent the risk of such an agency becoming industry-entrenched and lax, power should be given consumers to sue public officials who, through action or inaction, had shown a "reckless disregard for public health and safety."

By taking such action, we would be, as author Ralph Nader recently phrased it, "pioneering a sense of social values which does not think it necessary to wait upon disaster, recorded piles of corpses, or injured people before rational action is taken to foresee and forestall dangers. Prevention by legislative policy is preferable to belated legislative response in a nation that values human life and limb."

Chapter 6

The New Quackery

Although the old-time patent medicine man with his spiels for snake oil and other such nostrums has all but vanished from the American scene, medical quackery is far from a dwindling problem. It is, on the contrary, growing and becoming more dangerous, despite society's scientific advances. As Dwight L. Wilbur, M.D., then president of the American Medical Association, told participants at the AMA's most recent conference on quackery: "It is a puzzle that defies logical solution that in a nation where science had advanced to the point where we stand on the threshold of the moon, people will pay good money to sit on the dirt floor of a farmer's barn because he announces that radioactivity in his earth will cure cancer." Moreover as the nation grows more scientific, the quack adopts more pseudoscientific methods. It is not only the poor and uneducated who are vulnerable to quackery, pointed out another participant, but the "well-educated and sophisticated."

Today's quack has discarded the sinister black cutaway for the symbol of medical professionalism—the sterile white coat. He speaks knowledgeably of magnetism, vibrations, ionic effects, atoms, rays, cosmic radiation, trace minerals, organic foods, and often uses proper medical language. He bedecks his walls with framed diplomas, sometimes from legitimate schools, often from one of the country's two hundred diploma mills. Some quackery has become so sophisticated that it is supported by research studies and gargantuan advertising budgets. On the basis of "research" many reputable doctors and hospitals have bought and used diagnostic and therapeutic machines that were later proved worthless.

For this new quackery, Americans are paying at least one billion dollars a year, and according to one estimate by John Miner, former deputy district attorney of Los Angeles, two billion. That is more than we spend yearly for research on all disease and is enough to pay the Medicare tab for one year.

If the monetary costs of quackery are astronomical, the human costs are tragic and immeasurable. Millions of people, many sick and dying, trustingly place themselves in the hands of "doctors" who make a mockery of medicine and human dignity.

After Mrs. Lorraine Allen, a young New Jersey housewife stricken with rheumatoid arthritis, grew discouraged with her progress, she resorted to quack cures and was finally lured by an advertisement to one of the country's arthritis "clinics" for six weeks of treatment at $900. There she was taken off medically respected cortisone and subjected to chiropractic spinal manipulations, colonic irrigations, radiowave and ultrasonic treatments, massages and baths. Instead of improving, as the slick brochures had promised, Mrs. Allen grew worse day by day. "I had managed to walk into the clinic," she said, "but at the end of six weeks I was so sick and in such pain I could not leave. They told me I must stay for two more weeks, but even then they had to carry me out on a stretcher." Mrs. Allen was hospitalized, and after operations and physical therapy, her condition improved. Nevertheless, her fingers are drawn up in tight fists, and she is still in much pain. The two and a half years Mrs. Allen wasted on quackery have left her needlessly and permanently crippled.

In Spokane, Washington, a few years ago, Doris Hull, weighing only 108 pounds, was taken by her husband to a "sanipractor" named

Otis C. Carroll. Carroll claimed to be able to diagnose diseases by taking a drop of blood from a patient's ear and then placing the blood sample in a "radionics" machine. According to Carroll, Mrs. Hull's disease was minor. He prescribed hot and cold compresses and a ten-day fast, permitting her to take only water. Mrs. Hull's weight dwindled. Finally, weighing only 60 pounds, she died of starvation and tuberculosis, leaving both her husband and her child infected with tuberculosis.

Perhaps most heartbreaking of all is the case of eight-year-old Linda Epping, a beautiful blonde child who developed a small bump on her left eye which was diagnosed by doctors at UCLA Medical Center as cancer. Her parents were told the eye would have to be removed. While Linda was in the hospital awaiting operation, her parents learned of a chiropractor named Marvin Phillips, who claimed he could cure Linda without loss of the eye. They withdrew the child, and put her under Phillips's care at an initial fee of $500 and payments of $200 and $300 a month for medicine. Daily, the little girl was given vitamins, food supplements, laxatives, extract of beef eye (a daily dosage of 124 pills), and an iodine solution (11 glassfuls a day). During twenty-three days of this treatment, plus daily sessions of chiropractic manipulations, while Linda's parents watched, her eye grew steadily to the size of a tennis ball. Then Linda died. Said her grief-stricken mother who thought Phillips was a legitimate physician, "He had a nice shiny office, framed things on the wall, a lot of machines. How were we to suspect he was lying to us?"

Pondered deputy district attorney John Miner, who had seen Linda nine days before she died: "Except for the public executioner, only the medical quack is permitted to earn his living by killing people. . . . Whenever a quack guarantees a cure to a person who must have proper medical care to prolong or save life, he endangers that life. If his false representations keep the victim from the needed treatment until it is too late, he takes that life." To Miner, Linda's death was a case of murder. Indeed, Phillips was brought to trial in 1962, and despite a defense by the brilliant attorney, Melvin Belli, was convicted of murder. It was the first time in history a man had been condemned as a murderer for the practice of quackery, causing death. The verdict was appealed, and Phillips, on a legal technicality, was granted a new trial. In November 1967, he was convicted again of second degree murder.

The amount of human destruction due to quackery is impossible to ascertain. But Miner declares: "Quackery kills more people than those who die from all crimes of violence put together. It is public crime number one. I personally know of thirty instances in which the victims died as a result of relying on the fraudulent promises of quacks."

Three doctors at Duke University have reported that of sixty-four cancer patients referred to a hospital after being treated by quacks, twenty-seven died who might have lived if they had received proper treatment earlier. Ten of the patients who did survive were mutilated for life; some were left with bulging eyes and monstrous-size sores because the cancer had been allowed to grow unchecked. Others had their noses and mouths eaten away by the quacks' applications of strong caustics, which destroyed far more of the healthy tissue than would have been necessary in an operation. Only twenty-seven patients were fortunate enough to have forsaken the worthless remedies in time to avoid death or irreparable damage.

People turn to quacks out of desperation, seeking "miracle cures" and hope, often when none exists—which makes their situation all the more tragic. Not long ago a well-educated man walked into an office of the Arthritis Foundation wearing a cheap copper bracelet on his arm. "It's ridiculous, I know," he explained, "but I'm so desperate I'll try anything." Jerry Walsh, director of special services for the foundation, who was stricken with rheumatoid arthritis at age eighteen, admits that during the first seven and a half years of his illness, he spent $3,000 on quack cures, for everything from radium gadgets to "magic" buckeyes.

The American Cancer Society believes that testimonials, especially from friends and neighbors, or people who seem like friends and neighbors, are the most influential factor in convincing people to try quack cures. Some charlatans scribble off their own fictional testimonials. Others pay outright for signed letters of "Before I began taking Dr. X's miracle cure, I was a hopeless cancer victim." Recently, it was discovered that the glowing "return to health" testimonials widely distributed by one of the nation's arthritis "clinics" were written by college students, who earned part of their tuition by producing such harmful fiction.

Many testimonials, however, are voluntary and sincere. Dr. William Evans, then deputy director, Bureau of Medicine's Medical Review for the FDA, pointed out: "Quacks are always most 'successful' in treating diseases which have remissions and exacerbations—which come and go, periodically." Cancer has regressions. Arthritis flares up for inexplicable reasons, then may subside and leave the victim pain-free for months, even years. It has been reported that about one-fourth of all rheumatoid arthritics experience a "remission" after their first visit to a doctor or after taking their first nostrum. If a remission occurs at the same time as their adventure with quackery, they are convinced they have been cured. Undeniably, the placebo effect, as all doctors know, is also very strong. "Wave a wand over some patients, and they get well," says one FDA official.

Sometimes patients are misled into believing they are cured of a disease because of a false diagnosis. Some quacks call every mole, scar, or blemish "cancer"; then when it disappears or fails to grow worse, they claim to have cured it. Reputable physicians, too, can make a wrong diagnosis, opening the way for a quack to take credit for curing a disease that never existed.

Although authorities believe that most quacks are knowing scoundrels, testimonials can convince even them of their own healing powers. Says Irene Bartlett, quackery authority for the American Cancer Society: "It's understandable how some quacks begin to believe in the value of their own methods when they are constantly subjected to gratitude from people insisting they owe their lives to the 'doctor.'"

Like everything else in quackery, the testimonial has been revamped to fit modern medicine and technology. No longer does the testimonial travel from the medicine man's platform to a small crowd of fifty people. Through mass media it can reach millions.

Harry M. Hoxsey, first of the big-time charlatans in cancer cures, had a daily half-hour radio broadcast in the 1940s during which he presented the prize patients he had "cured" with his "secret combination of potassium iodide, licorice, red clover, burdock root, stillingia root, berberis root, poke root, cascara, Aromatic USP 14, prickly ash bark, buckthorn bark." Hoxsey, although he had only completed eighth grade, permitted himself the title of "Doctor" and established a nationally advertised cancer sanitarium in Dallas, Texas, where patients could receive the Hoxsey treatment for $400 plus $60 for X-rays and examination. Reportedly his income in 1951 was about $200,000.

A particularly attractive "cured" patient whom Hoxsey once paraded before a press conference was a little girl named Kathy Allison of South Bend, Indiana. A year later, at age six, Kathy died. Hoxsey attributed her death to pneumonia. It was true that a doctor, after a hasty diagnosis, had suggested the child might have pneumonia. But when the facts were explored further the truth was revealed. Clearly noted on Kathy's death certificate was "carcinoma" as cause of death. Several people who had forsaken operations for the Hoxsey method subsequently died. In at least one instance Hoxsey himself performed an operation. Using a razor blade, he cut open the breast of a woman and then packed the incision with an arsenic compound. The woman died ten days later of metals poisoning. In 1953, the FDA banned Hoxsey's "cure" from interstate commerce and in 1960 finally obtained a permanent injunction, closing his Texas clinic. The FDA found that not only was the Hoxsey remedy worthless, it could actually stimulate the growth of cancer. Nevertheless, the ubiquitous testimonials that keep Hoxsey's quack-remedy alive still appear in health magazines today.

The power of the testimonials and the mass media in selling quackery has perhaps never been more cynically displayed than in the case of Regimen reducing drugs.

Early in 1957, through national advertising, including commercials on Dave Garroway's "Today Show," Americans were alerted to the Regimen wonder drug, which promised immediate weight loss with no dieting whatever. Trumpeted the ads: "It's true! If you're normally healthy, you can lose as much as 70 lbs. without cruel diet, without giving up all your favorite foods." As living proof, overweight "housewives," supposedly taking Regimen, weighed in weekly on the "Today Show," cheerily vowing that all week long they had eaten potatoes, bread, rich desserts, and yet the pounds were falling away all because of Regimen. Some were losing as much as a pound a day right before the eyes of millions of viewers. It was convincing proof; sales shot up and by 1963, Americans had spent 16 million dollars for 4 million bottles of the colorful Regimen pills.

Extensive investigation by the FDA, the U. S. attorney's office in Brooklyn, and the U. S. Post Office revealed that the lovelies, sweetly praising Regimen before the cameras, were, when offstage, in teeth-gritting agony. They were not ordinary housewives; they were professional actresses. And they were on near-starvation diets of 500 calories daily; they were paid a fee for every commercial and a bonus for every pound they lost.

Regimen, as it turned out, was made up of three drugs, including ammonium chloride, a diuretic, and phenylpropanolamine, an appetite depressant. The former was in such weak dosage as to be inefficient, and the latter was totally ineffective. In other words, Regimen was a complete hoax. Yet, another amazing part of the Regimen story is that the efficacy of the drug was supported by four research studies, prepared by legitimate, and in two cases outstanding, researchers in medicine. In the new quackery, "substantiating product research" is a necessity; such research is the medicine man's wild claims clothed in the respectability of "science."

Through painstaking investigation, government officials dissected and then discarded the studies. Two were deceptively designed: in one, Regimen had been given to diabetics, and in another, to cardiac patients. The other two studies were good—too good. In truth, they were "graphite" studies; they had been written out without patients, without Regimen, without tests. Two well-respected researchers, holding thousands of dollars in research grants, supplied these falsified results in return for payments of $1,000 and $4,000 from the New Drug Institute, which was testing Regimen. One brilliant physiologist broke down and admitted that one evening she and a nurse had dashed off a study with fictional patients and fictional weight-loss.

In May 1965, the fraudulent merchants of Regimen were convicted in a federal district court in New York on twenty-five counts of criminal fraud. The Drug Research Corporation, the makers of Regimen, was fined $53,000; its president, John Andreadis, was fined $50,000 and sentenced to eighteen months in prison; and the New York advertising agency, Kastor, Hilton, Chesley, Clifford and Atherton, which prepared the phony TV commercials, was fined $50,000. It was the first time in history an advertising agency had been held criminally responsible for its participation in fraudulent huckstering.

Every trick of modern merchandising is used to exploit the hopes of the seekers-after-health. Busy canvassing the country are "doorbell doctors" who sometimes work a neighborhood in teams of two. One knocks on doors, hoping to find a person suffering from a serious disease. Since about 45 percent of all Americans have a chronic disease, his chances are not bad. Under the guise of conducting a "health survey" (Is anyone ill? Is he under a doctor's care?), he elicits the desired information. Later, his colleague, working another street, comes to the house offering quack cures. "I understand you have a diabetic living here," or arthritic, and so on. Thirty days or so after a sale, the salesman often checks back, asking how the medicine is working. If the victim says he is feeling better or the same, the salesman attempts to sell him other quack remedies to "cure you faster." Moreover, such hucksters exchange lists of customers; once a person buys, he is on the continuing quackery circuit, to receive not only salesmen, but dozens of publications and mailing pieces advertising health foods, wonder-clinics, and a variety of nostrums and devices.

High-pressure tactics are noticeably being used by some unscrupulous salesmen to sell shoddy hearing aids to the elderly. Numerous people are paying $350 and up for hearing aids that are not suited to their particular hearing loss. One man in California was sold an expensive hearing aid, which was completely useless: he had nerve damage. Others have been duped into paying $30 for useless rubber plugs, containing a small tuning fork, under the misapprehension that it would enable them to hear. The device costs thirty cents to make.

A man in Indiana recently wrote me:

"I am writing this to you to tell you how two old eighty-six- and eighty-one-year-old couples here were taken for $370 on a phony hearing aid deal by a ruthless hard-boiled high-pressure hearing aid salesman. . . . This is how he works. He knocks on the door. . . . I am Mr.____ sent to give you a free hearing test. . . . I am not going to tell you anything. . . . Then he took this machine into the kitchen, put it on the table, so he could test my hearing range. Then he turned some switches and knobs and put a hearing aid on my ear. He talked into the machine. The machine has a loudspeaker on it, but I didn't know it. Then he said I will give you a demonstration on how good our hearing aids are. He went into the next room. He was talking through the loudspeaker in the machine into my hearing aid. But I thought it was just his own voice. On the strength of this fake hearing aid demonstration I signed on the line, and was taken for $370." When the hearing aid came, the writer became suspicious and had his wife stand ten, then twenty, then fifty feet away and talk. "I couldn't hear her at all. Then I knew that the demonstration was a fake."

In the vicious world of big-business quackery, some entrepreneurs, as in other fields, have fashioned their practices to ensnare the poor. One of the most amazing commercializations in modern quackery operated in New York City, masterminded by Bernarr Zovluck, a chiropractor, who in 1969, was sent to prison for four years for mail fraud. The operation was a "clinic," directed by full-bearded "Dr." Zovluck, whose talents reportedly earn him an income of more than half a million dollars a year. Dr. Zovluck, whose talents also got him convicted for impersonating a physician in 1962, heads a staff of four chiropractors, one medical doctor, several white-uniformed nurses, and about thirty telephone operators, who occupy a whole floor in midtown Manhattan at Forty-second Street. On busy days, it is said that the clerks donned white coats and conducted physical examinations.

One room in the clinic was achatter with the voices of the thirty telephone solicitors scouring the city, mainly Harlem and the Puerto Rican district, for its poor and ill. Invitations were made for a "free medical examination at our clinic." Believing the clinic to be government-operated (some were led to believe it was a part of Medicare), people swarmed in, many feeble, some frighteningly ill and in need of professional care. Regardless of their ailments, they were routinely told they needed an X-ray (for which they paid a fee) and were put on Dr. Zovluck's multiple-treatment plan, costing $300 or $400, for which the patient-victim signed *an installment contract*. If the patient didn't find Dr. Zovluck's therapeutic plan beneficial (chiropractic manipulations and dietary restrictions) and refused to return or pay, the doctor, whom "God has chosen to help you get well," collected on the contract by having the patient's wages garnisheed. He also sent out intimidating dunning letters, headed "U. S. Credit Rating and Reporting Agency," reinforcing the notion that the clinic was government-run, and that if the patients didn't pay, the government would force them to.

The horror was that many people seeking help were genuinely ill. Stephen Press, then director of Massive Economic Neighborhood Development in Harlem, said that he knew of four persons who died and twenty who became seriously ill after being treated by Dr. Zovluck. In one case, an elderly man under Dr. Zovluck's care became progressively weaker over a period of four months. Alarmed, the man's daughter accompanied him to the clinic where she told Zovluck of her father's deteriorating condition. But the doctor, she says, insisted that the enfeebled man was fine, and was progressing nicely on a diet of fruit and liquid. Outside the building, the man collapsed and was rushed to Bellevue Hospital. Two weeks after entering the hospital, the man died.

Quackery, in both drugs and medical devices, is becoming more worrisome and difficult to control. Not only do old dangerous remedies and devices persist on the underground market, but new ones appear regularly. In the fast-moving world of medical discoveries where not even the experts agree, it is increasingly difficult to predict whether a "new miracle cure" will live up to its name or go down in history as another remnant of black magic.

Nowhere is the dilemma of the new quackery more evident than in drugs, especially those purporting to cure cancer. In keeping with the more sophisticated tenor of quackery, the American Cancer Society renamed its Quackery Committee the Committee on Unproven

Methods of Cancer Management. Its confidential list of "unproved methods" for treating cancer, many now being used throughout the country, contains nearly five hundred dubious remedies: among them are bamboo grass; mistletoe therapy; "Greendrink" (liquified herbs); the "Grape Cure"; the Hoxsey method; the Macrobiotic (or Zen) diet of rice cream, lotus roots, buckwheat bread, and tea; Diamond Carbon Compound; Laetrile; Koch antitoxins; Krebiozen; and the Rand Coupled Fortified Antigen.

Prominent among these was the Rand vaccine, which in 1966 was widely heralded as a possible new cancer cure. Based on the theory that cancer is caused by a virus, the anticancer vaccine was developed by the Rand Development Corporation, a private research organization in Cleveland, Ohio. It is claimed the vaccine builds up antibodies in the patient's blood which attack cancerous cells only. The antibodies are guided to their target by a hapten (a protein) which exists on the cell walls of tumors, but not on healthy cells. The antibody goes after this hapten, according to a Rand Corporation spokesman, shatters the cell wall, and destroys the tumor.

According to early testing on sixteen dying cancer patients, twelve reportedly were saved by the vaccine. As this news found its way into the press, it caused a sensation. Hope-filled patients and families begged doctors for the vaccine. In the fall of 1966, Rand's "broad-scale investigation" of the reputed cancer cure involved 75 doctors in 35 Ohio hospitals and 200 patients. By December, according to a trade newspaper, about 1,000 persons were receiving the vaccine.

Legally, the new vaccine could be tested only within the borders of Ohio. The Rand Corporation, under the 1962 Kefauver-Harris amendments, applied to the FDA for permission to test it in all fifty states as a new investigational drug. Under the law's provisions a company must show that the drug can be tested on humans with reasonable safety and effectiveness before it can be shipped across state lines. The Rand Corporation was unable to demonstrate that the vaccine was either reasonably safe or effective. They could not show that it met reasonable standards of quality or purity. Researchers had no adequate data to show that it was free of toxic side effects. They also failed to disclose that in one study of laboratory animals the vaccine had actually enhanced the growth of cancer. Thus, the FDA was forced to reject Rand's application for interstate distribution on the basis of insufficient data.

Nevertheless, Rand, without authorization, secretly shipped the vaccine to New York, Miami, and the West Coast. When vials of the vaccine were seized by the FDA, it was discovered that the vaccine had been manufactured under such substandard conditions of sanitation that it was contaminated with live bacteria. Because of the health risk as well as violation of the law, a federal court injunction was issued in March 1967 against the manufacture and distribution of the Rand vaccine in either Ohio or any other state until such time as the company is willing to do the preliminary research necessary to show that the vaccine has scientific validity and does not cause unreasonable risk to patients. Such an incident is truly regrettable, for it serves to darken rather than enlighten the way to a cancer cure.

Similarly, the controversial drug Krebiozen, which inflamed people's hopes for several years, was discredited, although its chief proponent was Dr. Andrew Ivy, a scientist of some reputation and a former vice-president of the University of Illinois. After investigation, the FDA branded Krebiozen "a cruel hoax," warning that "each day a person with treatable cancer relies upon Krebiozen is a day that brings him closer to death." In 1964, Dr. Ivy and three other persons using the drug, Dr. Stevan Durovic, Marko Durovic, and Dr. William Phillips, were tried in Chicago for mail fraud, violation of the Food, Drug and Cosmetic Act, and conspiracy. All were found not guilty. Nevertheless, Krebiozen, identified by the FDA as nothing more than creatine, a simple amino acid available in meat, cannot legally be sold across state lines. Despite the government's disapproval of the drug, many cancer victims are still receiving Krebiozen via underground sources.

As the experience with Krebiozen illustrates, once a remedy receives wide acclaim and attracts a number of supporters who believe they have been cured by it, suppressing its use is nearly impossible. Such "cures" persist for years. Laetrile, derived from the kernel of an apricot, has been around since the 1920s and has been branded "worthless." Yet its popularity comes and goes, and it is today one of the most popular among the underground cancer cures. Many persons cross the border into Mexico for treatments of laetrile, and recently California authorities arrested doctors prescribing laetrile. Its proponents urge that it be given scientific trials to determine its value, if any. The government has denied there is sufficient evidence of worth to warrant such trials.

For sheer tenacity, the Hoxsey "cure" cannot be matched. Now forty years old and completely denounced (one FDA official calls it "an outright fraud"), it is still being used on an alarming scale.

Especially disturbing in the marketplace of the new quackery is the illegitimate sale of potent drugs which, when properly used, do have legitimate purposes. Even the mail-order quack—the most small-time operator of all—has turned to peddling commercial drugs. When postal authorities investigated a recent scheme to treat epileptics by mail, they discovered the remedy was hardly a homemade honey and herb mixture; it was phenobarbital, cleverly promoted as a secret new drug. (Phenobarbital, besides being dangerous in large doses, is not accepted as a universal treatment for epilepsy.) Similarly, when California authorities looked into a direct mail piece promising rejuvenation, they did not find bottled water from Ponce de León's mythical fountain of youth. The liquid sold to "prolong mental and physical activities, as well as retard the symptoms of aging" was an injectible, called paraminobenzoic acid, a drug treatment from Rumania.

Also of grave concern to medical authorities are the so-called medical "devices" sold to detect and cure a dictionary of diseases such as bursitis, rheumatism, cancer, diabetes, heart disease, Bright's disease, tuberculosis, gout, insomnia, neuralgia, liver ailments, asthma, hepatitis, ear infections, skin diseases, brain tumors. A few are crude and relatively inexpensive: copper bracelets with "lifegiving properties," "magic crushed-rock amulets from Africa," health sandals, radium belts. But the majority are so well constructed and elaborate that they would not look out of place in a doctor's office. Most are expensive and bear pseudoscientific names, such as "microtabulometer," "Ionic charger," "Quot-Electronic Instrument," "Endocardiograph." In fiscal 1970, the Food and Drug Administration initiated more than 116 court cases involving such devices.

One of the most ingenious machine frauds was the Film-O-Sonic, an ordinary tape recorder from which the speaker had been removed. Wired to the machine were pads which the victim was to moisten and place against his body. The special vibrations from the silently playing tape were supposed to flow through the wires to the body, and in the case of cancer, seek it out and cause the tumor to disintegrate. When the tapes were played on a recorder with sound, the cancer "cure" was a rendition of "Smoke Gets in Your Eyes." The arteriosclerosis "cure" was "Holiday for Strings."

Although devices for home use account for millions of dollars worth of misery, far bigger business are the pseudoscientific contraptions that are used in the charlatan's "clinic" or "salon." Some of these cost thousands of dollars, but are a lucrative investment. One man in distress paid $28,000 to a quack for sessions with a machine that claimed to psychoanalyze him. For forty years, until her death in 1965 at the age of seventy-four, Ruth Drown, a chiropractor in Los Angeles, was the queen of modern machine quackery. Mrs. Drown was a disciple of Dr. Albert Abrams, an eminent cardiologist, who, early in the 1900s, with the advent of radio, became convinced that radio waves could both diagnose and cure all diseases. His theory was that every disease gives off radiations at a specified frequency, which can be measured on a "radionics" machine from a drop of a person's blood on a blotter. Once diagnosed, the disease is "cured" by broadcasting back into the sick patient at the same frequency emitted by the disease, thus destroying it by cancelling it out. Dr. Abrams charged patients $100 to $200 for a series of treatments on his numerous machines. He died in 1924, leaving an estate of 2 million dollars, a legacy of machine quackery, and a number of disciples, including Ruth Drown.

Mrs. Drown, a pert, grey-haired little lady, who dressed in professional white in her clinic, treated more than 35,000 persons in Los Angeles County alone, bilking them of at least half a million dollars. Her bungalow was given over to a clinic, full of about 125 machines. When Tyrone Power and his wife were injured in a plane crash in

Italy, Mrs. Drown claimed that she treated them by broadcasting her radionic vibrations for six thousand miles. So big was Mrs. Drown's business that handling it required, in addition to herself and her daughter, a staff of four nurses and a bookkeeper.

Finally, in 1963, Mrs. Drown and her daughter, Cynthia Chatfield, were indicted for grand theft. An undercover agent for the district attorney's office had sent Mrs. Drown a blood sample purporting to be that of a little girl. Mrs. Drown claimed the child had mumps and chicken pox. Actually, the blood sample came from a perfectly healthy turkey. Mrs. Drown died during the trial. Her daughter was convicted.

Some worthless machines are even finding their way into hospitals and physicians' offices. During a medical convention in 1958, physicians noted a marked similarity between the machines in an FDA quackery exhibit and a new machine called "Diapulse," being demonstrated in a nearby booth and offered for sale. After a lengthy investigation, the FDA, for the first time, took action against a so-called legitimate medical device being sold to reputable medical practitioners.

From 2,000 to 3,000 Diapulse machines were bought by medical practitioners and hospitals throughout the country for $2,300 each. The device was based on the medical theory of "pulsed diathermy," advanced in the 1930s and never widely accepted then. Theoretically, Diapulse's pulsating current penetrated deep into the body to the diseased organs, stimulating the body's production of antibodies and other defense mechanisms. According to the Diapulse Manufacturing Corp., its product accelerated healing in numerous ailments, including diabetic ulcer, arthritis ("effective where other treatment fails"), fractures, acute bacterial infections, upper respiratory infections, the common cold, acute tonsilitis, low blood pressure, and migraine headaches.

In a landmark case in 1967, a jury found Diapulse misbranded on forty-nine health counts, but the company continued to sell it with other health claims. As of mid-1971, the FDA was still trying to get a permanent injunction prohibiting sale of the device on the basis of *any* of its advertised health claims.

The FDA also moved against other medical devices not commonly considered quackery. The most notorious was Relax-A-Cizor, a muscle stimulator that bombarded the skin with tiny electrical charges that were supposed to destroy wrinkles, restore vitality, take off pounds. The FDA proved in court in 1970 that the device was both worthless as advertised and dangerous; it can damage the heart and other vital organs, induce miscarriages and possibly death. It is now banned in interstate commerce, but FDA officials fear similar muscle stimulators are being sold despite efforts to clamp down.

As the line between outright quack devices and those mistakenly used by men of some reputation draws ever finer, government officials are confronted with another unanticipated serious problem. Many devices are now implanted in the body—for example, artificial heart valves, synthetic arteries, metal leg plates, hip pins, joint prostheses. As medical science spurts ahead at fantastic speeds toward the "artificial man," we can expect to see humans equipped with even more vital artificialities: transistorized hearts, mechanical kidneys, and perhaps one day even artificial lungs and livers.

Such wonder devices could hardly be called quackery, for they have a legitimate health purpose and are implanted exclusively by licensed M.D.'s. Nevertheless, some of the prosthetic devices now being used skirt uncomfortably close to being termed quack in the sense that they are misrepresented, unreliable, a danger to health and, as the American Cancer Society would term it, "unproved" for their intended purpose.

Many prosthetic devices are subjected to scrupulous testing before marketing to be sure they are safe. But others are so irresponsibly made that they rust, break inside the patient and trigger biological reactions that cause infections and destroy tissue. In one instance, an elderly woman's broken hip was repaired with a nylon ball and metal pin. Within four months the woman's hip joint was completely destroyed. The nylon had reacted with the tissue, releasing a toxic material causing an abscess. Dr. Joseph Davis, director of medical devices of the FDA's Bureau of Drugs, has twenty-four different types of metal and plastic artificial eyes that were removed from patients because of defects in the material or poor design that caused severe tissue reaction and serious infection. In most cases, the tissue damage to the sockets was so extensive that the person could not be fitted with another artificial eye.

Breakage of metal hip pins and plates within a patient is extraordinarily common. Recently an engineer set up manufacturing in a California garage, turning out large metal nails designed to join the two parts of a broken hip. Within six months, there were three reported cases in a thirty-mile radius of the nails snapping in two after being imbedded in patients. Ironically this therapeutic hardware was advertised as being the strongest available. Said one ad: "Keeps Fracture Patient Up—Never Lets Him Down."

Metal screws, bone plates, and hip nails also corrode inside the patient. One surgical device, inserted as a hip pin, turned out to be an ordinary hardware store nail. Unless the metal is of a special type, biologically inert, it will create an electrolysis reaction, causing infection and pain, and will have to be removed.

FDA has a file drawer filled with reports of synthetic arteries rotting away inside patients, heart-pacemakers failing, aortic valves malfunctioning. Doctors at a prominent university recently found that of ninety-five patients who underwent operations for insertion of a graphite-coated heart valve, thirty-seven died. Two of the deaths were definitely traced to defective heart valves, and it was suspected, although not confirmed by autopsy, that other deaths were due to the heart valve. Several patients died of cerebral strokes. A question that went unanswered: Did bits of the graphite come off, creating an embolus that went to the brain, causing a fatal clot? In another study of seventeen cases, three patients died after the vital ball in their heart valve was expelled, and four others died because of valve leakage.

Unfortunately, under present laws, neither surgeons nor patients have protection from these defective, dangerously designed implants, which cause demonstrable harm and death. Anyone can make them and sell them. During Senate hearings before the Subcommittee on Frauds and Misrepresentations Affecting the Elderly in 1964, former Senator Ralph W. Yarborough of Texas questioned Dr. Martin Dobelle, at that time a medical officer for FDA.

Senator Yarborough: Now what protection does the surgeon have in introducing these pins into the human body? What protection has the surgeon got to know that the metals in these pins are the kind that have been made biologically inert and that they will not be hostile to human tissue?

Dr. Dobelle: Actually he has no protection whatsoever. Unfortunately, we have a gaining tide of malpractice suits, but counsel and attorneys in general now are aware of the fact that the defective device, even though the physician is a prime target, actually is the fault and the responsibility of the manufacturer.

Senator Yarborough: You mean . . . a competent surgeon introduces one of these pins into the body, to pin a broken hip, it is hostile, and the surgeon gets a suit for malpractice. There is no law or rule or regulation about the manufacture of these devices, these pins, these bolts, these metal braces that are put in the human body. There is no protection for the surgeon there except his judgment of the manufacturer; is that right?

Dr. Dobelle: That is correct, sir.

Surely all of these facts point to one disturbing conclusion: *that the public is not being adequately protected*—from either failure or misrepresentation of legitimate medical devices—and most decidedly, is not safeguarded from the purveyors of falsity who intentionally or unintentionally peddle suffering and death in the name of healing. Perhaps because we continue to think of the quack as a quaint crackpot in a top hat, we have been slow to recognize and to move against the horrors of modern quackery.

Most states actually license some quacks, legally entitling them to use the title "Doctor" or other titles of seemingly medical respectability: naturopath, naprapath, sanipractor, electrotherapist, scientologist, physiotherapist. If the quack does tangle with the law, he is often acquitted, or the sentence is suspended and the fine light —so light that many quacks laughingly refer to them as "license fees." When the redoubtable Mrs. Drown was convicted in federal court in 1951, after a woman had died from relying on one of her machines, she was fined $1,000, given a one-year suspended sentence and five years' probation. She continued her business without interruption, and in 1963 when arrested bragged: "The advertising will be good for me. When I get back to my office, I'll have more patients than ever."

A distributor of a quack radon generator, selling for $300, was fined $25. A "Doctor" who had treated nearly 1,000 patients on his "Electrometabograph" machine at fees as high as $1,500 was fined $750. After an elderly lady suffering from advanced tuberculosis was discovered in a third-rate hotel sitting on a radium pad to cure her "arthritis," the several vendors were apprehended and fined. Seldom did the fine exceed the profit from *one sale*.

Most quacks enjoy a lifetime of comfort, free from the law. But, if their businesses are shut down, they move easily from state to state. Before coming to New York City to prey on Harlem's sick, Dr. Zovluck ran a clinic in Baton Rouge, Louisiana, with a staff of two hundred. Roy Wright DeWelles, a long-time quack, operated a clinic in Los Angeles until 1961. He used a pressurized enema device called a "Detoxacolon," which he claimed flushed out the colon, removing toxins which caused all ailments, including cancer, asthma, arthritis, colitis, epilepsy. Such an instrument can perforate colon walls, remove vital body salts, and spread infections. An investigation by the California State Department of Health revealed that more than 13 percent of DeWelles's patients died after his treatments. The state closed down the clinic; DeWelles was brought to trial but acquitted. Within the following year he had organized one of his infamous "traveling clinics" in Indiana, using the same dangerous Detoxacolon. This time, however, an Indianapolis judge, deploring the light sentences that allow quacks to continue to operate, sentenced DeWelles, then age sixty-one, to ten years in prison. It was one of the stiffest sentences ever given to a medical con man.

Nevertheless, during his long, lucrative career, DeWelles had sold at least two hundred Detoxacolon devices to other practitioners for $2,500 each. The FDA managed to find and destroy only a few of these potentially deadly machines. Nearly all of the original two hundred may still be in use today—and perhaps will be until subsequent deaths bring the machines to the attention of law officials.

What needs to be done?

1. Of urgent importance is federal legislation to prevent unsafe and worthless medical devices from being marketed, and several Congressmen have introduced such bills. It is sad and wasteful that year after year we stand by helplessly while dangerous and ineffective medical devices are sold, and then make futile, costly attempts to remove them from the market *after they have caused harm.* It is shameful that the public, through taxes, bears the financial burden of simply halting *further* marketing of the devices—by means of FDA seizures, FDA administrative and FDA-requested court proceedings. Prosecution of a recent case alone cost an estimated $250,000.

Moreover, FDA's after-the-fact action does not rid the country of devices already sold. As in the case of the dangerous Detoxacolon, the devices continue to be used long after their makers are forced out of business. The FDA seizures, except in extreme cases of health-danger, are not designed, as many believe, to remove misbranded devices from the market. Often only one seizure of a misbranded medical device is made, as a prerequisite for legal action. Only one Diapulse machine was seized, for example. The other 2,999 or so, as far as anyone knows, are still in use.

We do not allow drugs to be tested on humans to determine if they are safe and efficacious. Nor should we allow this kind of inhuman experimentation and exploitation by medical devices. The makers of medical devices, like those of drugs, should be required to supply sound scientific evidence that their product is safe and effective for its intended uses *before* the government allows it to be marketed.

The Kefauver-Harris Amendments of 1962, requiring the drug premarketing clearance, originally included the same provisions for medical devices, but this aspect of the bill was lost in the battle over drugs. Similar medical device legislation was introduced in 1966, 1967, 1969, and 1971, but did not create much of a stir, despite presidential endorsements. Obviously, with each passing year, need for the law becomes more pressing. We must prevent any new saturation of the country with such patently fraudulent diagnostic and therapeutic devices as the Drown machines, the ozone generators, the Sonic Tape Recorders. (Some would exclude from the law diagnostic devices, but it seems to me some of these are the most dangerous of all and should not be granted immunity.)

Perhaps more important for the future—and this is the main thrust of the legislation—it would for the first time set uniform standards for the manufacture of legitimate medical devices, such as the heart valves, hip pins, and mechanical miracles to come. Both patients and surgeons deserve the assurance that these human implants are as safe as they can be made.

2. An Anti-Quackery Bureau should be established in the Department of Health, Education and Welfare. Throughout the country, on federal, state, and local levels, hundreds are working tirelessly to curtail quackery, but as John Miner, the Los Angeles prosecutor, observed, "The right hand rarely knows what the left hand does." There is no national clearing house for information on quackery. Quacks can skip all over the country before the FDA or the postal officials hear of their existence. An FDA study of five hundred medical devices showed that FDA officials did not even learn of the violations in most cases until months, sometimes years, had passed. One wrist device to "cure" arthritis was on the market in 1892, but was not removed by FDA until 1958.

A national anti-quackery bureau would provide a center for information, to be exchanged among federal agencies, local officials, private health organizations, and the public. By coordinating both enforcement and educational activities nationwide through the bureau, we could for the first time present a formidable united front against the evils of quackery.

3. States should pass anti-quackery legislation and enforce it vigorously. Although a sizable percentage of the nation's quackery takes place within state borders, few states have adequate laws to handle it. Thirteen states do not even have a basic, comprehensive food, drug and cosmetic act, which would empower them to take the same action locally as the FDA can take nationally. The Council of State Governments has drawn up model food and drug legislation and urges all states to adopt it. Such legislation provides an essential groundwork for fighting quackery.

Few states that do have comprehensive laws have updated them to require the premarket testing of drugs to parallel the 1962 federal drug amendments. And, only California, in a law passed in 1962, has raced ahead of the federal government to require that new medical devices be determined safe and worthwhile before they can be sold.

California, plagued with an overpopulation of quacks, and sometimes called the "Mecca of Quackery," can also be called the "Land of Anti-Quackery." That state is and should be emulated for its progressive anti-quackery laws and vigorous pursuit of quacks. In 1959, California was the first to pass a special cancer control law, under which the state can issue regulations banning cancer remedies found by a fifteen-member council of experts to be unproved. The law enables authorities to move swiftly to remove old, persistent quack cures, such as the Hoxsey remedy, without having to bring lengthy court proceedings. Anyone found selling one of the outlawed cancer remedies can be immediately forbidden to do so, under a cease and desist order, and if necessary, with a court injunction. Seven other states also now have cancer antiquackery laws, based on California's. They are Colorado, Kentucky, Maryland, Nevada, North Dakota, Ohio, and Pennsylvania. The American Cancer Society urges all states to pass such legislation and has drawn up a model law to facilitate passage and uniformity.

In 1967, California, in an unprecedented hard crackdown on quacks, raised the crime of practicing medicine without a license from a mere misdemeanor, subject to a maximum $500 fine and six months in jail, to a felony, which carries a possible prison sentence of ten years.

In addition to considering these laws, it seems to me states should reexamine their medical licensing procedures and be quicker to revoke the licenses of quacks, and perhaps refuse to grant licenses to pseudomedical practitioners at all. South Carolina, for example, recently outlawed naturopaths, after the State Medical Society brought pressure and the brother of a state legislator had tragically died at the hands of a naturopath. The FTC has also urged states to follow Oregon's lead in licensing hearing aid dealers and salesmen. Sellers would be required to pass an examination for competency, and in the case of misbehavior, their licenses could be revoked.

State medical boards, as well as local and national medical groups, might also take a more stringent approach to censuring and revoking the licenses of their members who indulge in quackery. Although it is a serious move to jeopardize a man's livelihood, it is even more serious to allow him to jeopardize the lives of others. If I, as a practicing lawyer, consistently refused to follow the established rules of the court, I would expect to be quickly disbarred. A continued faith in the medical profession is essential to defeating quackery.

However, no matter how much people respect and trust their own doctors, those who hold out false hopes of miracle cures—of an easier, faster, better way to relieve pain, cure illnesses, and prolong life—will always find a pathetically eager market. We must marshal every force, including strong, stringently enforced laws, to stop modern-day quacks from such cynical exploitation of the gullible and the desperate.

Chapter 7

Toward a Safer Cigarette?

For the last several years, especially since the Surgeon General's Smoking and Health Report of 1964, we have referred to the danger of cigarettes as the "smoking controversy." Millions of Americans have refused to face the grim fact that they may be smoking themselves into an early grave. And the tobacco industry has steadfastly questioned the evidence that links cigarettes with disease and death, clinging to every last hope and maverick voice in the research wilderness that might release their product from blame.

In scientific truth, there is no longer any "controversy." Since the surgeon general's definitive report, hundreds of other studies have confirmed that cigarette smoking is linked to a number of diseases. In the laboratories cigarette tar painted on the backs of mice has induced cancer. Dogs and rabbits, taught to smoke through machines, have developed precancerous lung changes and emphysema. The clinical evidence is even more indisputable. A recent autopsy study of the cross sections of human lung tissue revealed that 93.2 percent of the smokers had abnormal lung cells as compared with

161

only 1.2 percent of the nonsmokers. In a study of one million men and women, Dr. E. C. Hammond of the American Cancer Society found that male smokers between the ages of forty-five and sixty-four had a death rate from all causes that was twice as high as that of nonsmokers.

Perhaps the most dramatic single piece of evidence of the causal relationship between smoking and lung cancer is the experience of British physicians. In 1951 the percentage of male English doctors smoking cigarettes was 56 percent. Alarmed by the demonstrated health hazards, many doctors gave up cigarettes. By 1958 only 40 percent of the British doctors smoked cigarettes. As the lung cancer rate among the general public in Great Britain rose by 25 percent between 1954–57 and 1962–64, the lung cancer rate among doctors dropped by 7 percent.

The magnitude of the health problem from smoking is enormous. As former Surgeon General William H. Stewart has pointed out, fifty years ago lung cancer was a rare disease; today it is increasing at epidemic proportions. In 1930, deaths from lung cancer in the United States totaled 2,500. This year about 60,000 American men and women will die of the disease, 50,000 primarily as a result of cigarette smoking. (Smokers are ten times more likely than non-smokers to die of lung cancer.) By 1976, unless the epidemic is checked, 80,000 yearly will die of the disease.

More Americans die from heart disease than from any other disease. Every year a million people in this country have heart attacks or die suddenly from coronary heart disease. There are several manifestations of coronary heart disease, all related in part to atherosclerosis—a disease in which fatty materials accumulate in the walls of medium or large arteries. Cigarette smoking is an important risk factor in the development of coronary heart disease and, by accelerating damage already present as a result of coronary heart disease, may contribute to sudden death. In the total male population, the death rate from coronary heart disease averages 70 percent higher for smokers compared to nonsmokers. Men between the ages of forty-five and fifty-four who are heavy smokers have coronary heart disease death rates three times higher than those of nonsmokers, and women in the same age group who are heavy smokers have coronary heart disease death rates twice those of nonsmoking women.

Bronchopulmonary diseases—principally emphysema and chronic bronchitis—have also been increasing at an alarming rate. In 1955, 4,000 persons died of emphysema or bronchitis, a slow suffocating death. By 1964, the number of deaths from emphysema and bronchitis had risen to more than 20,000.

Only two years later, deaths from these diseases had risen another 25 percent. Cigarette smoking is now considered to be the most important cause of chronic bronchitis—more important than air pollution. The exact cause of emphysema is less clear, but it is thirteen times more likely to strike smokers than nonsmokers. Even more disturbing than the death rate for smokers chalked up by these diseases is their devastating role as cripplers of men and women. Many are forced to retire during their most productive years because of these diseases.

Confronted with such scientific data, what can we do and what are we doing to curb the toll from cigarettes?

Our first effort was to pass legislation requiring the familiar "Caution: Cigarette smoking may be hazardous to your health" on every package. But we were soon told by public health officials that the warning was inadequate. The warning was a symbolic gesture of government disapproval (American Cancer Society posters warned: "Congress has acted. The next step is up to you.") but it is doubtful that the message made many converts. And our efforts were lamentably small when pitted against the industry's monumental expenditures for cigarette advertising. While the government was warning against smoking, the tobacco companies in 1968 spent 310 million dollars, more than two-thirds of it on television commercials, which conveyed the impression that smoking was satisfying, pleasurable, socially desirable, and not harmful to health.

Thus, it became increasingly apparent that stronger measures were necessary. In 1969 Senator Frank E. Moss of Utah and myself stepped in and set legislation on a course that ended in passage of the Public Health Cigarette Smoking Act of 1969. It called for (1) an end to all broadcast cigarette advertising by January 1, 1971; (2) a strong warning on cigarette packages: "Warning: The Surgeon General has determined that cigarette smoking is dangerous to your health"; and (3) it left the FTC free to act on cigarette advertising in nonbroadcast media in accordance with the agency's powers over advertising, subject to a six-month delay for Congressional review.

Although it is a relatively brief time since all sections of the 1969 act have been implemented, unquestionably the legislation was a constructive effort to reduce the effect of cigarette smoking without banning the product entirely. Subsequently, the cigarette industry agreed to display the warning on the package in all advertisements. One of the major cigarette manufacturers, however, refused to do so. The FTC then issued a complaint against American Brands, Inc., as well as against other cigarette manufacturers who did not display the warning in cigarette advertisements clearly and prominently.

But in spite of these meager industry efforts, which are magnanimous compared to actions and practices conducted in past years, the cigarette industry has spread its promotion tactics to innumerable other markets, and in its zeal to keep up consumption has, using new methods, begun pandering to women and children.

The 240 million dollars formerly spent on radio and TV advertising has been transferred, by and large, into the print media. And in addition to broadening their appeal in special interest publications, the cigarette industry seems bent on infusing the smoking habit into every man, woman, and child.

A quick review of recent issues of several magazines demonstrates the insidious inroads into the home which the tobacco industry has succeeded in making. Although there are a number of publications which do not take any cigarette advertising, namely, the *Boston Globe*, the *Christian Science Monitor*, the *New Yorker*, *Good Housekeeping*, *Readers Digest*, and the *Saturday Review*, many publications continue to reap the benefits of the Congressional ban on broadcast advertising. The conscience of these publications must be very shallow, indeed so shallow as to ask whether they demand any standards whatsoever other than a high credit rating. For these advertisements are solicitations to death.

The September 1971 *Woman's Day*, a publication sold primarily

at supermarkets, shows five full pages, one half page, and the back
cover, all in full color inviting the modern homemaker to smoke.

An elegant woman in evening gown appears in a Kool advertisement in which the copy suggests, "Come all the way up to Kool
Filter Longs. Stylishly long, tastefully cool. Lady Be Cool."

Clad in high suede boots, hot pants, and a cloche, the Virginia
Slims model beckons women to join her, "You've Come a Long Way
Baby." The catchy broadcast advertising jingle and slogan almost
sings out of the printed page, playing quite consciously in the readers' ears.

The handsome coffee drinking model in the Kent advertisement
beckons with "Coffee 'n Kent! What a good time for all the good
things of a Kent."

With seductively pretty package graphics that carry onto the cigarette itself, we read "Farewell to the ugly cigarette. Smoke Pretty.
Eve." The copy goes on to extol the virtues of smoking a cigarette
truly created for women: "Hello to Eve. The first truly feminine
cigarette—it's almost as pretty as you are. With pretty filter tip.
Pretty pack. Rich, yet gentle flavor. Women have been feminine
since Eve. Now cigarettes are feminine. Since Eve."

And Viceroy beckons women smokers, depicting a cocktail party
featuring an attractive young model: "Parties? She loves 'em. Meets
interesting people that way. Music? Anything from Bach to rock. Her
cigarette? Nothing short of Viceroy Longs. She won't settle for less."

The back cover? Of course, another cigarette advertisement, a
scene picturing a young couple in a country store with the slogan
"Winston's Down Home Taste."

The September 10, 1971, issue of *Life* and the September 21, 1971,
issue of *Look* seem representative of this trend with four full pages
and ten full pages, respectively.

But the appeal of the advertisements appearing in the general interest or family magazines is definitely toward the young people. At
the House hearings on cigarette labeling and advertising, one industry witness testified that sweepstakes, coupons, and premiums were
more of an attraction to young people than cigarette advertising.
Tareyton is represented by a premium and Winston by a sweep-

stakes, and Raleighs and Belair by coupon promotions, in the current issues of *Life* and *Look*.

Additionally, the tar and nicotine content of some of the lower brands on the tar and nicotine scale is used as a selling point to the thousands of health conscious smokers who have been unable to quit but are still concerned for their health. Philip Morris Multifilter offers a cigarette "Lower in tar than 95 percent of all cigarettes sold. Full Kentucky flavor in a low-tar cigarette." True counters with "True is lower in both tar and nicotine than all other cigarettes sold . . . in fact, True is lowest in both tar and nicotine of the 20 best-selling brands. That's why True puts its numbers on the front of every pack."

But in spite of the implicit evidence in these advertisements that cigarettes are a health hazard, and the explicit display of the health warning in most of these advertisements, the tobacco industry moguls, represented in Washington by the Tobacco Institute, Inc., continue to spend thousands of dollars trying to convince themselves and the public that cigarettes may not be hazardous. Indeed, the Tobacco Institute propaganda would have the public believe that the evidence which has been turned up by hundreds of medical researchers in thousands of studies is motivated by a moral persuasion which finds cigarettes a public nuisance.

The Tobacco Institute has published advertisements, put on speakers led by the physicians and statisticians used at the Congressional hearings, distributed propaganda under the signature of others, and even produced two prosmoking television spot announcements which it has tried to convince broadcasters to run.

Between 1966 and 1970, cigarette consumption in the United States progressively decreased. Contrary to the impression created by cigarette advertising, only 42 percent of adult men and 31 percent of adult women are still smoking cigarettes; the rest have either managed to quit or never took up the habit in the first place. The change is very significant considering that in 1966, 52 percent of adult men and 34 percent of adult women smoked.

Smoking among teen-agers, however, has been increasing. Exactly why this is taking place is not fully understood; it may be a temporary phenomenon. Teen-agers are more likely to smoke if one or both parents or an older brother or sister smokes. They are more likely to smoke if one or both parents are absent from the home. The attitudes and behavior of their friends are obviously very important in a youngster's decision to smoke. As a rule, teen-agers smoke far less than adults. Many of them, particularly the younger ones, smoke only two or three cigarettes a week.

In 1970, Americans paid out approximately 11 billion dollars or 2 percent of the income they had left after taxes for tobacco products, that was 2½ times the dollar value of tobacco purchases in 1950, largely due to increases in prices and tobacco taxes. But per capita use of cigarettes has fallen from a high of 4,345 per person in 1963 to about 4,000 during 1970.

A ban on all advertising may prove highly desirable—*unless* we can by regulation and education make advertising work to stimulate the sale of less hazardous cigarettes. This is the other half of the picture. But whatever we do, millions will continue to smoke. And we should turn some attention toward making the cigarette itself less hazardous to lessen the toll of death and disability. For we do know how to produce less hazardous cigarettes.

Although we don't have all the answers about why and how smoking causes damage, it is increasingly evident that tar, the brownish black residue which is left after the smoke is demoisturized or "condensed," is a significant factor. Studies on both animals and humans reveal that the higher the dose of tar and nicotine (which is a particular substance in tar), the greater the danger to health. For example, mice subjected to twice as much tar developed twice as many tumors. Smokers who turn to cigarettes with a lower tar-nicotine content show significantly less coughing and shortness of breath than those who stay with higher tar-nicotine brands. A study in 1967 by Saxon Graham, at the State University of New York in Buffalo, demonstrated that smokers develop individual techniques of smoking, and that those who smoke in such a way as to extract the greatest amounts of tar from their cigarettes appear to have the highest incidence of lung cancer. (Taking the same number of puffs over a longer period of time, allowing the cigarette to burn down reducing filtration length, and puffing more at the end of the cigarette rather than at the beginning yielded the largest amounts of tar.)

The harmful effects of nicotine are also documented. According to Dr. Hammond, "Milligram for milligram, nicotine is one of the most powerful and fastest acting of all known poisons. However, when an amount which would produce rapid death if administered in a single dose is split into many small doses and administered during the course of the day, the effects are very different."

Nicotine and carbon monoxide appear to be important factors in the mechanism that produces coronary heart disease. Nicotine increases the demand of the heart for oxygen and other nutrients, while carbon monoxide decreases the ability of the blood to furnish needed oxygen.

Within this framework of the hazards of the nicotine, tar, and gas phase of tobacco smoke, most notably carbon monoxide, efforts must be made to reduce the intake.

Those smokers who have not yet been able to quit, can at least cut down. One way they can do this is by smoking low tar and nicotine cigarettes. Cigarettes are now on sale with tar levels of four milligrams and nicotine levels below 0.3 milligrams, but so far these are not large sellers. Most Americans buy cigarettes with considerably higher levels than these.

There are five suggestions that the smoker can follow if he wants to make his smoking habit a less hazardous one. They are taken from a Public Health Service publication entitled "If You Must Smoke." The suggestions are: inhale less, smoke fewer cigarettes, take fewer puffs, smoke only half-way down, and choose a low tar and nicotine cigarette.

It is a good idea to smoke only half-way down because tobacco acts as a filter, retaining a portion of the tars and nicotine that pass through it. The farther down the cigarette burns, the greater is the tar and nicotine dose. The first half of the cigarette yields only about 40 percent of the total tar and nicotine, the second half about 60 percent.

We are not on the threshold of an absolutely safe cigarette, nor do we know if it is possible to produce a perfectly safe cigarette that anyone would care to smoke. Millions of dollars, however, are going into research toward a safer cigarette in many places, including the laboratories at the U. S. Department of Agriculture; Sloan-Kettering Institute for Cancer Research in New York City; the Veteran's Administration Hospital in East Orange, New Jersey; Roswell Park Memorial Institute near Buffalo, New York; and even in the laboratories of the cigarette manufacturers themselves, although they are reluctant to admit it.

We do not know nearly enough about the actual biological causes of smoking-induced death: which of the many chemicals in tar produce the damage and how; whether toxic gases given off by smoke, such as carbon monoxide, cyanide, and hydrogen sulfide, contribute to the harm. Thus, we must pursue all areas which will further our knowledge of the hazard. However, we do right now have compelling evidence that tar-nicotine causes harm in proportion to its content, and that by reducing the tar-nicotine, we can reduce the health danger. We need not wait longer for research in this area. We must immediately take measures to decrease the dose of tar per cigarette and to warn the public of the tar danger in particular brands.

There is a wide range in tar content. The Federal Trade Commission's semiannual tests for August 1971 showed that tar yielded by cigarettes ranged from four milligrams per cigarette (Carlton, Marvels, and Sano) to thirty-three milligrams (Players). It was also apparent that some filters are not filtering out the tar particles effectively. The range in tar recovery from filters was four milligrams per cigarette (Carlton, Marvels, and Sano) to thirty milligrams per cigarette with Bull Durham king size filter. Generally the amount of tar depends on two factors: the length of the cigarette—the longer it is the greater total amount of tar; and the weight of the filter —heavier, more dense filters (with a harder draw) trap more of the tar particles. Failure to produce low tar-nicotine cigarettes is not due to lack of technology. Tar and nicotine researchers at Roswell Park Memorial Institute have concluded, "It seems clear that manufacturers are able to produce cigarettes with almost any yield of tar and nicotine from very low to very high."

Moreover, we are beginning to accumulate data on which brands actually are associated with the greatest incidence of cigarette-caused disease and death.

The dissemination of information on relative hazards by brand name has forced cigarette companies to lower the tar-nicotine yield of some of their products as a matter of competitive survival. It is hardly likely that Americans will deliberately buy the highest tar-producing cigarettes when they are told the comparative dangers. The enormous swing to filters illustrates that American smokers are health conscious. Within the last fifteen years filters have captured 75 percent of the market. Since the spring of 1966, P. Lorillard Company's True has become a major brand, the first of the low tar-nicotine cigarettes to succeed. Sales are also up for the low tar-nicotine Carltons, Cascades, and Marvels.

In general, cigarettes are slowly becoming less hazardous; the cigarette of 1966 on the average contained about two-thirds as much tar and nicotine as the average cigarette in 1960.

Nevertheless, the hazard is of such magnitude that we cannot depend only on competition and the sporadic consciences of tobacco companies to reduce the tar-nicotine to necessary levels for the protection of health, as manufacturers have proved by their excursion into the 100 millimeter field. Therefore, I have also formulated legislation which will gradually, over a period of years, substantially reduce the dangerous tar-nicotine of cigarettes. The Federal Trade Commission would be empowered to set maximum permissible tar and nicotine yields for all cigarettes sold in the United States. We do not know, nor are we likely to know in the near future, what levels, if any, of tar and nicotine can be considered safe. But we can at least eliminate those cigarettes, including many of the 100 millimeters, which are unconscionably lethal in the tar-nicotine output in the light of present knowledge.

Realistically, we cannot suddenly effect by legislation a drastic across-the-board decrease in tar levels, for it is evident that many Americans are so addicted that the "withdrawal symptoms" might be intolerable, and a black market for high tar-nicotine cigarettes might spring up with an attendant criminality and a breakdown in law as it did during Prohibition. Rather, under the FTC's direction, manufacturers should be permitted to reduce the tar-nicotine levels of each of their brands gradually, until the low permissible level has been reached. Over several years, the tar-nicotine yields would be lowered to a relatively innocuous dosage without undue distress to smokers.

Of course all of our efforts would be canceled out if, in response, smokers simply began smoking more cigarettes to obtain a desired quota of tar. Studies show that this does not happen; those who switch to low tar and nicotine cigarettes generally smoke the same number as their old brand, and often fewer. The switch to low tar-nicotine cigarettes also is not infrequently a first step toward quitting.

The design of the filter appears to be one method of reducing the tar-nicotine output. Filters that effectively filter are immediately available and in use on some brands. Generally, these filters remove particles of tar on a nonselective basis—the tighter the filter, the more particles of tar it catches. Eventually, it might be possible to filter out only those substances of the tar which cause the harm, but at present we do not know which of the specific tar agents are dangerous. The filter can also be designed to prevent the smoking of the cigarette down to a small butt. The final puffs on a cigarette contain much more tar than the initial puffs because the tobacco-filtering length of the cigarette has been decreased steadily with each puff. A longer filter or a longer paper overwrap would automatically cut off the burning and delivery of tar at a critical stage, preventing smokers from obtaining that last lethal dosage of tar. Tobacco companies could also select less lethal tobacco by choosing leaves from the lower part of the stalk which are known to contain less tar-nicotine than those at the top.

As long as cigarette sales continue to soar, the tobacco industry will regard health warnings as an annoyance—of little consequence. It is clear that for the protection of the health of American consumers, Congress must once again, as we must in the areas of hazardous products and quackery, take strong decisive action in stemming the flow of dangerous products into the marketplace by striking at the source—in this case, by modifying the cigarette itself.

Appendix

Brand	Type	Tar (mg/cig)	Nicotine (mg/cig)
Carlton	reg. size, filter	3	0.2
Sano	reg. size, filter	4	0.2
Marvels	king size, filter, menthol	4	0.2
Carlton	king size, filter	4	0.4
Marvels	king size, filter	5	0.2
King Sano	king size, filter	6	0.3
King Sano	king size, filter, menthol	6	0.2
Life	100 mm, filter	10	0.6
Frappe	king size, filter, menthol	10	0.3
Kent	reg. size, filter	10	0.6
Tempo	king size, filter	12	0.9
Vantage	king size, filter	12	0.8
True	king size, filter	12	0.6

Brand	Type	Tar (mg/cig)	Nicotine (mg/cig)
Multifilter	king size, filter, menthol (plastic box)	12	0.9
True	king size, filter, menthol	13	0.7
Doral	king size, filter	14	0.9
Doral	king size, filter, menthol	14	1.0
Sano	reg. size, nonfilter	15	0.5
Silva Thins	100 mm, filter, menthol	16	1.1
Parliament	king size, filter (hard pack)	16	1.0
Multifilter	king size, filter (plastic box)	16	1.1
Parliament	king size, filter	16	1.0
L & M	reg. size, filter	16	1.0
Silva Thins	100 mm, filter	16	1.1
Kent	king size, filter	17	1.0
Eve	100 mm, filter	17	1.2
Kent	king size, filter	17	1.0
Lark	king size, filter	17	1.0
Pall Mall	95 mm, filter, menthol (hard pack)	17	1.2
L & M	king size, filter (hard pack)	17	1.1
Eve	100 mm, filter, menthol	17	1.1
Belair	king size, filter, menthol	17	1.3
Virginia Slims	100 mm, filter	17	1.1
Viceroy	king size, filter	17	1.2
Raleigh	king size, filter	17	1.2
Montclair	king size, filter, menthol	17	1.3
DuMaurier	king size, filter (hard pack)	18	1.2
Raleigh	100 mm, filter	18	1.3
Oasis	king size, filter, menthol	18	1.1
Virginia Slims	100 mm, filter, menthol	18	1.2
Viceroy	100 mm, filter	18	1.3
Edgeworth Export	king size, filter (hard pack)	18	1.2
Edgeworth Export	100 mm, filter, menthol	18	1.3
Lark	100 mm, filter	18	1.2
Alpine	king size, filter, menthol	18	1.2
Benson & Hedges	reg. size, filter (hard pack)	18	1.3
Pall Mall	100 mm, filter, menthol	18	1.4
Kool	king size, filter, menthol	18	1.4
Marlboro	king size, filter, menthol	18	1.1
Vogue (colors)	king size, filter (hard pack)	18	0.7
New Leaf	king size, filter, menthol	19	1.3
Chesterfield	king size, filter, menthol	19	1.1
Pall Mall	95 mm, filter (hard pack)	19	1.3
Chesterfield	king size, filter	19	1.2
Edgeworth Export	100 mm, filter	19	1.3
L & M	100 mm, filter, menthol	19	1.2
Belair	100 mm, filter, menthol	19	1.4
Kent	100 mm, filter, menthol	19	1.1

Brand	Type	Tar (mg/cig)	Nicotine (mg/cig)
Peter Stuyvesant	king size, filter	19	1.4
L & M	100 mm, filter	19	1.3
Pall Mall	100 mm, filter	19	1.3
Salem	king size, filter, menthol	19	1.3
Newport	king size, filter, menthol (hard pack)	19	1.1
Kool	100 mm, filter, menthol	19	1.4
L & M	king size, filter	19	1.3
Marlboro	king size, filter (hard pack)	19	1.3
Chesterfield	101 mm, filter	19	1.3
Tareyton	king size, filter	19	1.3
Kent	100 mm, filter	19	1.2
Parliament	100 mm, filter	19	1.3
Picayune	reg. size, nonfilter	19	1.3
Winston	king size, filter	19	1.3
Tareyton	100 mm, filter	19	1.3
Home Run	reg. size, nonfilter	19	1.3
Winston	king size, filter (hard pack)	20	1.3
Camel	king size, filter	20	1.3
Salem	100 mm, filter, menthol	20	1.3
Maryland	100 mm, filter, menthol	20	1.3
Domino	king size, filter, menthol	20	1.3
Marlboro	king size, filter	20	1.3
Peter Stuyvesant	100 mm, filter	20	1.5
Benson & Hedges	king size, filter (hard pack)	20	1.4
Winston	100 mm, filter	20	1.3
Galaxy	king size, filter	20	1.4
Newport	king size, filter, menthol	20	1.1
Old Gold Filters	king size, filter	20	1.2
Benson & Hedges	100 mm, filter, menthol	21	1.4
Benson & Hedges	100 mm, filter	21	1.4
Kool	reg. size, nonfilter, menthol	21	1.3
Winston	100 mm, filter, menthol	21	1.5
Newport	100 mm, filter, menthol	21	1.2
Marlboro	100 mm, filter (hard pack)	21	1.5
Domino	king size, filter	21	1.3
Marlboro	100 mm, filter	22	1.5
Spring	100 mm, filter, menthol	22	1.1
Lucky Filters	100 mm, filter	22	1.6
Old Gold Straights	reg. size, nonfilter	22	1.2
Lucky Filters	king size, filter	22	1.6
Mapleton	king size, filter	23	1.1
Marvels	king size, nonfilter	23	0.8
Piedmont	reg. size, nonfilter	24	1.3
Old Gold Filters	100 mm, filter	24	1.5
Half & Half	king size, filter	24	1.7

Brand	Type	Tar (mg/cig)	Nicotine (mg/cig)
Philip Morris	reg. size, nonfilter	24	1.5
English Ovals	reg. size, nonfilter (hard pack)	25	1.8
Camel	reg. size, nonfilter	25	1.5
Chesterfield	reg. size, nonfilter	25	1.5
Mapleton	reg. size, nonfilter	25	1.0
Raleigh	king size, nonfilter	26	1.6
Vogue (black)	king size, filter (hard pack)	27	0.9
Domino	king size, nonfilter	27	1.4
Old Gold Straights	king size, nonfilter	28	1.5
Lucky Strike	reg. size, nonfilter	29	1.7
Herbert Tareyton	king size, nonfilter	29	1.8
Pall Mall	king size, nonfilter	29	1.8
Chesterfield	king size, nonfilter	29	1.7
Philip Morris Commander	king size, nonfilter	29	1.8
Bull Durham	king size, filter	30	1.9
English Ovals	king size, nonfilter	30	2.2
Fatima	king size, nonfilter	32	1.9
Players	reg. size, nonfilter	33	2.4

Bibliography

Much of the source material for this book came from personal knowledge, communications, and interviews. However, the reader who would like to explore the subject further has available a number of excellent sources. The authors found the following articles, books, and other publications especially valuable in preparing this book.

Part One

Amount of Earnings Exempt from Garnishment under State Laws. U. S. Department of Labor, Bureau of Statistics, July 1967.

"Are Changes Coming in Those One-Sided Credit Laws?" *Consumer Reports,* XXXI (Mar. 1966), 108–12.

Armbrister, Trevor, "Land Frauds: The Ads Promise Wonders But Look Before You Buy." *Saturday Evening Post* (Apr. 27, 1963), 17–22.

Berton, Pierre, *The Big Sell.* New York: Alfred A. Knopf, 1963.

Bivens, Gordon E., *The Spender Syndrome: Case Studies of Sixty-Eight Families and Their Consumer Problems,* ed. by Brenda Dervin. Milwaukee, Wisconsin: University of Wisconsin Center for Consumer Affairs, 1965.

Borrie, Gordon J., and Diamond, Aubrey L., *The Consumer, Society and the Law,* rev. ed. London: MacGibbon and Kee, Ltd., 1966.

Brunn, George, "Wage Garnishment in California: A Study and Recommendations," 53 *Calif. L. Rev.* 1214 (1965).

Caplovitz, David, "On the Value of Consumer Action Programs in the War on Poverty." Office of Economic Opportunity, Mar. 8, 1966.

———. *The Poor Pay More: Consumer Practices of Low-Income Families.* New York: Free Press, 1963.

The Challenge of Crime in a Free Society. Washington, D. C.: Report by the President's Commission on Law Enforcement and Administration of Justice, 1967.

Consumer Issues '66. Washington, D. C.: Report to the President from the Consumer Advisory Council, 1966.

Consumers' Voice. Philadelphia: Consumers' Education and Protective Association monthly newspaper, 1966–67.

Curran, Barbara A., *Trends in Consumer Credit Legislation.* Illinois: University of Chicago Press, 1965.

"Developments in the Law–Deceptive Advertising," 80 *Harv. L. Rev.* 1005 (1967).

Fact Booklet Series. Boston: Better Business Bureau Educational Division.

First Annual Report on Justice and the Poor of Washington State. Seattle-King County: Legal Services Center, Feb. 1967.

"Fraud: Victims Frightened by Legal Threats." *The Evening Star,* Washington, D. C., Aug. 30, 1966.

Gentry, Curt, *The Vulnerable Americans.* Garden City, New York: Doubleday and Company, Inc., 1966.

Gotschall, Gale P., "Help! Help! or Why FTC Seeks Aid of the Attorneys General in Combatting Consumer Deception and Unfair Competition." Santa Fe, New Mexico: Remarks before the

Western Conference, National Association of Attorneys General, Sept. 2, 1966.

———. "How the Federal Trade Commission Can Work with Businessmen and Prosecutors." Tampa, Florida: Remarks before the First Annual Seminar, Florida Council on Commercial Frauds, Feb. 18, 1967.

———. "Let's Join Hands to Prevent Consumer Deception." Remarks before the National District Attorneys Association, June 6, 1966.

Jones, Commissioner Mary Gardiner, "Deception in the Marketplace of the Poor: The Role of the Federal Trade Commission." Washington, D. C.: Remarks before the Zonta Club, June 22, 1966.

———. "Our Most Urgent Task: To Protect the Consumer Needs of Our Poverty-Stricken Families." Miami, Florida: Remarks before the Spring Community Forum "Women on the Move" of the Greater Miami Section, National Council of Jewish Women, Inc., Apr. 22, 1966.

Kiernan, Gladys, ed., *1966 Retailers Manual of Laws and Regulations*. Oct. 1966.

Lefkowitz, Louis J., *Report of Bureau of Consumer Frauds and Protection*. New York: Department of Law, State of New York, 1966.

McMaster, John B., *History of the People of the United States from the Revolution to the Civil War*, ed. by Louis Filler. New York: Farrar, Straus and Co., 1964.

Mindell, Stephen, "The New York Bureau of Consumer Frauds and Protection—A Review of its Consumer Protection Activities," 11 *New York Law Forum* 603 (1965).

1965 Law and Poverty. Washington, D. C.: Report of the National Conference on Law and Poverty, June 23–25, 1965.

O'Connell, John J., "The Art of Losing Money," Seattle, Washington: Remarks before the 34th Annual Convention, Washington Credit Union League, Apr. 14, 1967.

———. "Consumer Protection in the State of Washington." *State Government*, XXXIX (Autumn 1966), 230–39.

———. "Highlights of Consumer Protection Legislation Passed by
the 40th Session Washington State Legislature." Report for the
Washington State Labor Council AFL–CIO, Tenth Annual Convention, Aug. 28–31, 1967.

Ora Lee Williams v. Walker-Thomas Furniture Co., 350 F2d 445.

*People of Illinois, ex rel. William G. Clark v. Raymond E. Hackler
and Richard Burkholder, d/b/a Burkholder and Hackler, and
Raymond E. Hackler, Richard E. Burkholder and Theodore
"Ted" Hatfield as individuals,* Circuit Court of Cook County,
Illinois, 63 C 4565.

Peterson, Mrs. Esther, "Equality in the Marketplace." Los Angeles,
California: Remarks before the National Conference of the NAA-
CP, July 7, 1966.

Proceedings: 57th Annual Meeting. National Association of Attorneys General, Dec. 1963.

Proceedings: 59th Annual Meeting. National Association of Attorneys General, Dec. 1965.

*Public Hearings of the Subcommittee of the New York State Fi-
nance Committee.* Mar. 9, 1967.

"The Regulation of Advertising," 56 *Colum. L. Rev.* 1018 (1956).

"A Salesman Says." *Home Furnishings Daily,* July 14–28, 1958.

Sand, Michael A. and Weisburg, Joel, "Translating Sympathy for
Deceived Consumers into Effective Programs for Protection,"
114 *Pennsylvania L. Rev.* 395 (1966).

Schur, Jerome, "A Study of Consumer Credit Legislation." Municipal Division of the Circuit Court of Cook County, Illinois, 1966.

Sherwood and Roberts-Yakima, Inc. v. Leach, 409 2d 160 (1965).

Smith, Ralph Lee, "Saga of the Little Green Pig." *Reporter* (Nov.
3, 1966), 39–42.

State by Lefkowitz v. ITM, Inc., 275 NYS 2d 303.

United States of America before the Federal Trade Commission:
In the Matter of Allied Enterprises, Inc., a corporation, and
William Marion, individually, and as an officer of said corpora-
tion. Docket No. 8722.

United States of America before the Federal Trade Commission:
In the Matter of The Empeco Corporation, a corporation, d/b/a

Empire Furniture and Appliance Co., and as Empire Home Improvement Co., and Allen C. Baverman, individually, and as an officer of said corporation. Docket No. 8702.

United States of America before the Federal Trade Commission: In the Matter of Holland Furnace Company. Docket No. 6203.

United States of America before the Federal Trade Commission: In the Matter of John A. Guziak, an individual trading as General Aluminum Company, a corporation, and as Superior Improvement Company, a corporation. Docket No. 8614.

U. S. Congress. House. Committee on Banking and Currency. *H. R. 11601, Consumer Credit Protection Act.* Hearings before the Subcommittee on Consumer Affairs, 90th Cong., 1st Sess. (Aug. 7, 8, 9, 10, 11, 14, 15, 16, 17, 18, 1967).

U. S. Congress. Senate. Committee on Banking and Currency. *S. 275, Interstate Land Sales Full Disclosure Act of 1967.* Hearings before the Subcommittee on Securities, 90th Cong. 1st Sess. (Feb. 28, Mar. 1, 1967).

U. S. Congress. House. Committee on Post Office and Civil Service. *H. R. 1411, to Amend Title 39, United States Code, with respect to Use of the Mails to Obtain Money or Property under False Misrepresentations.* Hearings before the Subcommittee on Postal Operations, 90th Cong., 1st Sess. (Apr. 12, 1967).

U. S. Congress. Senate. Committee on Post Office and Civil Services. *S. 274, to Amend Sec. 4005, Title 39, United States Code, Relating to Fraudulent, False or Misleading and Lottery Mail.* Hearings before the Subcommittee on Postal Affairs, 90th Cong., 1st Sess. (Aug. 15, 1967).

U. S. Congress. Senate. Special Committee on Aging. *Health Frauds and Quackery: Eye Care.* Hearings before the Subcommittee on Frauds and Misrepresentations Affecting the Elderly, 88th Cong., 2nd Sess. (Apr. 6, 1964).

U. S. Congress. Senate. Special Committee on Aging. Subcommittee on Frauds and Misrepresentations Affecting the Elderly. *1964 Investigations, Findings, Recommendations: 1964 Report.* 1965 (89th Cong., 1st Sess. Committee Print.)

Weston, Glen E., "Deceptive Advertising and the Federal Trade Commission: Decline of Caveat Emptor," 24 *Federal Bar Journal* 548 (1964).

Part Two

Accident Facts. National Safety Council. 1967.

Bylinsky, Gene, "The Search for a Safer Cigarette." *Fortune* (Nov. 1967), 146–49, 200, 202, 204, 206, 209.

Carper, Jean, "At Last—Clothing That Won't Burn." *Family Safety,* XXIV (Spring 1965), 10–13.

———. *Stay Alive!* Garden City, New York: Doubleday and Company, Inc., 1965.

Consumer Reports, 1963–1967.

"Crackdown on Quackery." *Life,* LV (Nov. 1963), 72B–83.

"Estimates of Injuries Associated with Products, Equipment and Appliances in the Home Environment." Injury Control Program, Public Health Service, Department of Health, Education and Welfare, Aug. 18, 1966.

"Facts on Glass Door Safety." Architectural Aluminum Manufacturers Association, Sept. 6, 1967.

Facts on Quacks—What You Should Know About Health Quackery. American Medical Association Department of Investigation, 1967.

FDA Report on Enforcement and Compliance, 1963–1966.

Graham, Saxon, Ph. D., "Lung Cancer as Related to Smoking Behavior Patterns." Paper presented at the American Public Health Association, Oct. 26, 1967.

Grant, Roald N., M. D., and Bartlett, Irene, *Unproven Methods of Cancer Treatment.* American Cancer Society, Inc., 1966.

"Health Characteristics by Geographic Region, Large Metropolitan Areas and Other Places of Residence." *Vital and Health Statistics,* National Center for Health Statistics, U. S. Dept. of Health, Education and Welfare, Ser. 10, No. 36 (July 1963–June 1965).

Hedrick, Dr. James L., "Facts on Smoking, Tobacco and Health." Draft prepared for National Clearinghouse for Smoking and

Health, Public Health Service, Dept. of Health, Education and Welfare. Bethesda, Maryland: Resource Management Corporation, Sept. 1967.

Horn, Daniel, Ph. D., "How Did Society Get Into the Cigarette Mess? Why Is It So Hard to Find a Way Out?" New York: World Conference on Smoking and Health, Sept. 12, 1967.

Kaplan, Jack, "Doctor Abrams—Dean of Machine Quacks." *Today's Health* (Apr. 1966), 21, 70–73, 77–80.

Magnuson, Warren G., "Establishment of a National Commission on Product Safety." *Congressional Record* (Feb. 8, 1967), S. 1755–1758.

———. "Flammable Fabrics Act Amendments." *Congressional Record* (Feb. 16, 1967), S. 2037–2038.

———. "Introduction of Amendments to the Cigarette Labeling and Advertising Act." *Congressional Record* (May 17, 1967), S. 6975–6983.

———. "Power Lawn Mower Safety." *Congressional Record* (July 23, 1965), 17380–17382.

———. "Strengthening the Cigarette Labeling Act." *Congressional Record* (July 27, 1966), 16467–16474.

Manchester, Harland, "What You Should Know About Flammable Fabrics." *Reader's Digest,* XC (May 1967), 37–38, 40.

McConnell, William H. and Knapp, L. W., "Epidemiology of Rotary Power Lawn Mower Injuries." *Bulletin No. 9,* Institute of Agricultural Medicine, Dept. of Preventive Medicine and Environmental Health, College of Medicine, University of Iowa, 1965.

Meserve, William G., "Cigarettes and Congress." California: Remarks before the California Conference on Cigarette Smoking and Health, Oct. 29, 1967.

Miner, John, "The Phillips Case—A New Dimension in Murder." *Journal of Forensic Sciences,* IX (Jan. 1964).

Moore, George E., M. D., Ph. D., Bros, Irwin, Ph. D., Shamberger, Raymond, Ph. D. and Bock, Fred G., Ph. D., *Tar and Nicotine Retrieval from Fifty-Six Brands of Cigarettes.* Buffalo, New York: Roswell Park Memorial Institute (New York State Department of Health), 1967.

Nader, Ralph, "The Engineer's Professional Role: Universities, Corporations, and Professional Societies." *Engineering Education* (Feb. 1967), 450–54.

Neuberger, Maurine B., *Smoke Screen: Tobacco and the Public Welfare.* Englewood Cliffs, New Jersey: Prentice-Hall, Inc., 1963.

"The 100 mm. Mess." *Tobacco Reporter,* XC (Oct. 1967), 20–24, 62.

Press, Edward, M. D., "Wringer Washer Machines Injuries." *American Journal of Public Health,* LIV (May 1964), 812–22.

"The Price of Faulty Design Gets Steeper Every Day." *Product Engineering* (Aug. 1, 1966), 34–43.

Proceedings: National Congress on Medical Quackery. Sponsored by the American Medical Association and the Food and Drug Administration, Oct. 6–7, 1961.

Proceedings: 2nd National Congress on Medical Quackery. Sponsored by the American Medical Association and the Food and Drug Administration, Oct. 25–26, 1963.

Proceedings: 3rd National Congress on Medical Quackery. Sponsored by the American Medical Association and the Food and Drug Administration, Oct. 7–8, 1966.

Report to Congress Pursuant to the Federal Cigarette Labeling and Advertising Act. Federal Trade Commission, June 30, 1967.

Stewart, William H., M. D., "Keynote Address: Influencing Smoking Behavior." New York: World Conference on Smoking and Health, Sept. 12, 1967.

Textile Flammability Conference. Boston, Massachusetts: National Fire Protection Association International, Oct. 2–3, 1962.

Underwriters' Laboratories Report of Electrical Accidents. Jan.–Nov., 1966.

USA v. Bernarr Zovluck, Alvin Eisenstein and Anne Friedman, U. S. Dist. Crt., Southern Dist. of N. Y., Indictment 73 CR 513.

U. S. Congress. Senate. Committee on Commerce. *S. 2507 and S. 2508, Overhead and Underground Transmission Lines.* Hearings before the Committee, 89th Cong., 2nd Sess. (May 4, 1966).

U. S. Congress. Senate. Committee on Commerce. *S. 3298, Child Protection Act of 1966.* Hearings before the Consumer Subcommittee, 89th Cong., 2nd Sess. (Aug. 24, 26, 1966).

U. S. Congress. Senate. Committee on Commerce. *S. J. Res. 33, to Establish a National Commission on Products Safety.* Hearings before the Consumer Subcommittee, 90th Cong., 1st Sess. (Mar. 1, 1967).

U. S. Congress. Senate. Committee on Commerce. *S. 1003, to Amend the Flammable Fabrics Act.* Hearings before the Consumer Subcommittee, 90th Cong., 1st Sess. (May 3, 4, 5, 1967).

U. S. Congress. Senate. Committee on Commerce. *Report on Flammable Fabrics Act Amendments of 1967.* 90th Cong., 1st Sess. (July 25, 1967).

U. S. Congress. Senate. Committee on Commerce. *S. 2067, Radiation Control for Health and Safety Act of 1967.* Hearings before the Committee, 90th Cong., 1st Sess. (Aug. 28, 29, 30, 1967).

U. S. Congress. Senate. Committee on Commerce. *To Review the Progress Toward the Development and Marketing of a Less Hazardous Cigarette.* Hearings before the Consumer Subcommittee, 90th Cong., 1st Sess. (Aug. 23, 24, 25, 1967).

U. S. Congress. Senate. Special Committee on Aging. *Frauds and Quackery Affecting the Older Citizen.* Hearings before the Committee, 88th Cong., 1st Sess. (Jan. 15, 1963).

U. S. Congress. Senate. Special Committee on Aging. *Health Frauds and Quackery.* Hearings before the Subcommittee on Frauds and Misrepresentations Affecting the Elderly, 88th Cong., 2nd Sess. (Jan. 13 and Mar. 9, 1964).

U. S. Congress. Senate. Special Committee on Aging. Subcommittee on Frauds and Misrepresentations Affecting the Elderly. *1964 Investigations, Findings, Recommendations: 1964 Report.* 89th Cong., 1st Sess. Committee Print. (1965).

U. S. Congress. Senate. Special Committee on Aging. *Consumer Interests of the Elderly.* Hearings before the Subcommittee on Consumer Interests of the Elderly, 90th Cong., 1st Sess. (Jan. 17, 18, 1967).

U. S. Congress. House. Committee on Post Office and Civil Service. *H. R. 6102 to Amend Sec. 4005, Title 39, United States Code, Relating to Fraudulent, False or Misleading and Lottery Mail.*

Hearings before the Subcommittee on Postal Operations, 89th Cong., 2nd Sess. (June 7, 1966).

U. S. Public Health Service. *The Health Consequences of Smoking: A Public Health Service Review: 1967.* Washington, D. C.: U. S. Department of Health, Education and Welfare, 1967.

Walrad, Ruth, *The Misrepresentation of Arthritis Drugs and Devices in the United States.* New York: Arthritis and Rheumatism Foundation, 1960.

White, William V., *Accidental Injuries Associated with Rotary Lawn Mowers.* Outdoor Power Equipment Institute in cooperation with the National Safety Council, n.d.

———. *Preventing Burns from Clothing Fires: The Public Health Approach.* Public Health Service, U. S. Department of Health Education and Welfare, and the National Fire Protection Association, n.d.